HEAVEN

RANDY ALCORN

with learning activities by Dale McCleskey

LifeWay Press®
Nashville, TN

ISBN 1-4158-3219-6

The book is a resource in the Bible Studies category of the
Christian Growth Study Plan. Course: CG-1229

Dewey Decimal Classification: 231.7
Subject Headings: GOD \ HOLY SPIRIT \ SPIRITUAL LIFE

To order additional copies of this resource: WRITE LifeWay Christian Resources Customer Service; One LifeWay Plaza; Nashville, TN 37234-0133; FAX order to (615) 251-5933; PHONE (800) 458-2772; ORDER ONLINE at *www.lifeway.com;* E-MAIL *orderentry@lifeway.com;* or VISIT the LifeWay Christian Store serving you.

Art Director: Jon Rodda
Cover Photography: Michael W. Rutherford, Rutherford Studios
Interior Design: Susan Browne Design

Printed in the United States of America

Leadership and Adult Publishing
LifeWay Church Resources
One LifeWay Plaza
Nashville, TN 37234-0175

CONTENTS

About the Authors

RANDY ALCORN is the founder and director of Eternal Perspective Ministries (EPM). He served as a pastor for 14 years. He has spoken around the world and has taught on the adjunct faculties of Multnomah Bible College and Western Seminary.

Randy is the best-selling author of 23 books including the novels *Deadline, Dominion, Deception, Lord Foulgrin's Letters,* and the Gold Medallion winner *Safely Home.* His 14 nonfiction works include *Money, Possessions and Eternity, ProLife Answers to ProChoice Arguments, In Light of Eternity, The Treasure Principle, The Grace & Truth Paradox, The Purity Principle, The Law of Rewards, Why ProLife?, Heaven, Questions and Answers about Heaven* (for 8-12 year olds), and *50 Days of Heaven* (meditations on Heaven).

Randy has written for many magazines and produces the popular periodical Eternal Perspectives. He's been a guest on over 500 radio and television programs.

The father of two married daughters, Randy lives in Gresham, Oregon, with his wife and best friend, Nanci. They are the proud grandparents of three grandsons, Jacob, Matthew, and Tyler. Randy enjoys hanging out with his family, biking, tennis, research, and reading.

DALE MCCLESKEY wrote the learning activities for the study. He is an editor in chief for undated resources at LifeWay. He is the husband of Cheryl, father of Jason and Jodi, and grandfather of Autumn and Amber. He has written or contributed to more than 25 books.

Introduction

by Dale McCleskey

I first encountered Randy Alcorn through his excellent fiction. Among other titles, if you haven't read *Safely Home, The Edge of Eternity, Deadline*, or *Dominion*, you're missing a treat. We at LifeWay have partnered with Randy to produce studies like *The Treasure Principle, The Purity Principle*, and *The Grace & Truth Paradox*. When I read *Heaven*, I knew this was a book that had to become a group study. As a writer and editor at LifeWay, I've worked on many great biblical studies with many well-known authors. I can't think of any I have personally been more committed to or excited about than *Heaven*.

Everyone needs an anchor. Unfortunately most people—Christians included—have dropped anchor in the shifting sands of this world. With every tide change of pop culture, their moorings drift and shake.

Everyone needs an anchor, but unless it's resting firmly in the right foundation, we're just hauling heavy chains for nothing.

The little flock of believers in Luke 12:32 had chains too, but their anchors rested in the world to come. When trouble came, their anchors provided stability through all of life's storms. How can the world shake a person whose treasure rests securely in a land this age cannot touch?

Early Christians were preoccupied with Heaven. The Roman catacombs, where the bodies of many martyred Christians were buried, contain tombs with inscriptions such as:

- In Christ, Alexander is not dead, but lives.
- One who lives with God.
- He was taken up into his eternal home.

One historian writes, "Pictures on the catacomb walls portray Heaven with beautiful landscapes, children playing, and people feasting at banquets."

In A.D. 125, a Greek named Aristides wrote to a friend about Christianity, explaining why this "new religion" was so successful: "If any righteous man among the Christians passes from this world, they rejoice and offer thanks to God, and they escort his body with songs and thanksgiving as if he were setting out from one place to another nearby."

These early Christian perspectives sound almost foreign today, don't they? But their beliefs were rooted in the Scriptures.

In this book we'll see an exciting yet strangely neglected truth—that God never gave up on His original plan for human beings to dwell on earth. In fact, the climax of history will be the creation of New Heavens and a New Earth, a resurrected universe inhabited by resurrected people living with the resurrected Jesus (Rev. 21:1-4).

In these pages I want to encourage you to place your anchor firmly in Heaven, where it can yield a reward of faithful stability in your life. I want us to be so excited about Heaven that we will have maximum effectiveness in this present world. I desperately desire that same stability and effectiveness for you. Thank you for joining in this journey of Bible study.

Several actions will help you benefit most from this interactive study. First, though the study can be done alone, your journey will be greatly enhanced by a group. If you haven't already become part of a Bible study group, I encourage you to gather some friends and do the study together. Include in your group those who have not yet met Christ. It's a great way to reach out. Sheila Moss has written the leader guide to help you conduct a group study. It begins on page 147.

Second, do not just read over the activities. You will see that many of them call for personal sharing. I wish we could sit down together and talk about Heaven. Randy would love to hear your stories and celebrate your victories. Since that may have to wait, please let these pages be our sharing time. You will see that we've laid out the study in daily portions to help you develop your habit of Bible study.

Finally, I want to explain that we at LifeWay have distilled this study from the 500-page hardback book. So where Randy may have shown several Scriptures for a particular point, this workbook may show only one or two. Where he may have explained a point with multiple illustrations, the study only lists one. If you have questions, or want more explanations, please consult the larger version. Information about the larger book appears on page 160. This workbook does contain the central teachings of the book in a more group friendly form.

Thank you for joining us in a quest to reclaim our heritage. When our anchor clings to God's eternal promise, we can stand through anything this world can throw at us. Most of all, we can sacrifice for a time when we see our reward.

Dale McCleskey

Realizing Our Destiny

Are You Looking Forward to Heaven?

Many people find no joy at all when they think about Heaven.

A pastor once confessed to me, "Whenever I think about Heaven, it makes me depressed. I'd rather just cease to exist when I die. I can't stand the thought of that endless tedium. To float around in the clouds with nothing to do but strum a harp ... it's all so terribly boring. Heaven doesn't sound much better than hell. I'd rather be annihilated than spend eternity in a place like that."

Where did this Bible-believing, seminary-educated pastor get such a view of Heaven? Certainly not from Scripture, where Paul said to depart and be with Christ was far better than staying on earth (see Phil. 1:23). My friend was more honest about it than most, yet I've found that many Christians share the same misconceptions about Heaven.

After reading my novel *Deadline,* which portrays Heaven as a real and exciting place, a woman wrote me, "I've been a Christian since I was five. I'm married to a youth pastor. When I was seven, a teacher at my Christian school told me that when I got to Heaven, I wouldn't know anyone or anything from earth. I was terrified of dying. I was never told any different by anyone. … It's been really hard for me to advance in my Christian walk because of this fear of Heaven and eternal life."

Let those words sink in: "This fear of Heaven and eternal life."

Referring to her recently transformed perspective, she said, "You don't know the weight that's been lifted off of me. … Now I can't wait to get to Heaven."

How do you feel about Heaven? (Check all that apply.)
❑ I'm so excited about Heaven I can hardly stand it.
❑ I just don't think about Heaven at all.
❑ I fear Heaven.
❑ I'm dreading Heaven.
❑ Could we talk about something else, please?

OUR UNBIBLICAL VIEW OF HEAVEN

When a colleague asked an English vicar what he expected after death, he replied, "Well, if it comes to that, I suppose I shall enter into eternal bliss, but I really wish you wouldn't bring up such depressing subjects."[1]

Over the past 15 years I've received thousands of letters and have had hundreds of conversations concerning Heaven. I've spoken about Heaven at churches and conferences. I've written about Heaven and taught a seminary course titled "A Theology of Heaven." There's a great deal I don't know, but one thing I do know is what people think about Heaven. And frankly, I'm alarmed.

WHERE DO WE GET OUR MISCONCEPTIONS?

I believe there's one central explanation for why so many of God's children have such a vague, negative, and uninspired view of Heaven: the work of Satan.

Jesus said of the Devil, "When he lies, he speaks his native language, for he is a liar and the father of lies" (John 8:44). Some of Satan's favorite lies are about Heaven. Revelation 13:6 tells us the satanic beast "opened his mouth to blaspheme God, and to slander his name and his dwelling place and those who live in heaven." Our enemy slanders three things: God's person, God's people, and God's place—namely, Heaven.

What benefits do you think Satan hopes to get from teaching us to dread Heaven?

_____

_____

_____

After being evicted from Heaven (see Isa. 14:12-15), the Devil became bitter not only toward God but also toward mankind and toward the place that was no longer his. It must be maddening for him that we're now entitled to the home he was kicked out of. What better way for the Devil and his demons to attack us than to whisper lies about the very place on which God tells us to set our hearts and minds?

Satan need not convince us that Heaven doesn't exist. He need only convince us that Heaven is a boring, unearthly place. If we believe that lie, we'll be robbed of our joy and anticipation, we'll set our minds on this life and not the next, and we'll not be motivated to share our faith. Why should we share the "good news" that people can spend eternity in a boring, ghostly place that even we're not looking forward to?

Satan hates the New Heaven and the New Earth as much as a deposed dictator hates the new nation and new government that replaces his. Satan cannot stop Christ's redemptive work, but he can keep us from seeing the breadth and depth of redemption that extends to the earth and beyond. He cannot keep Christ from defeating him,

> Our enemy slanders
> God's person,
> God's people,
> and God's place.

but he can persuade us that Christ's victory is only partial, that God will abandon His original plan for mankind and the earth.

Because Satan hates us, he's determined to rob us of the joy of believing what God tells us about the magnificent world to come.

So How Can We Correct Our Inaccurate Ideas About Heaven?

When Jesus told His disciples, "In my Father's house are many rooms ... I am going there to prepare a place for you" (John 14:2), He deliberately chose common, physical terms (house, rooms, place) to describe where He was going and what He was preparing for us. He wanted to give His disciples (and us) something tangible to look forward to—an actual place where they (and we) would go to be with Him.

This place is not an ethereal realm of disembodied spirits—humans are not suited for such a realm. A *place* is by nature physical, just as humans are by nature physical. (We are also spiritual.) What we are suited for—what we've been specifically designed for—is a place like the one God made for us: earth.

In this study we'll see from Scripture an exciting yet strangely neglected truth—that God never gave up on His original plan for humans to dwell on earth. In fact, the climax of history will be the creation of a New Heaven and a New Earth, a resurrected universe inhabited by resurrected people living with the resurrected Jesus (Rev. 21:1-4).

"Do not let your hearts be troubled. Trust in God; trust also in me. In my Father's house are many rooms; if it were not so, I would have told you. I am going there to prepare a place for you. And if I go and prepare a place for you, I will come back and take you to be with me that you also may be where I am." JOHN 14:1-3

SEEING THE SHORE

Perhaps you've come to this study burdened, discouraged, depressed, or even traumatized. Perhaps your dreams—your marriage, career, or ambitions—have crumbled. Perhaps you've become cynical or have lost hope. A biblical understanding of the truth about Heaven can change all that.

In 1952 young Florence Chadwick stepped into the waters of the Pacific Ocean off Catalina Island, determined to swim to the shore of mainland California. She had already been the first woman to swim the English Channel both ways. The weather was foggy and chilly; she could hardly see the boats accompanying her. Still, she swam for 15 hours.

When she begged to be taken out of the water along the way, her mother, in a boat alongside, told her she was close and that she could make it. Finally, physically and emotionally exhausted, she stopped swimming and was pulled out. It wasn't until she was on the boat that she discovered the shore was less than half a mile away. At a news conference the next day she said, "All I could see was the fog. ... I think if I could have seen the shore, I would have made it."[2]

Consider her words: "I think if I could have seen the shore, I would have made it." For believers, that shore is Jesus and being with Him in the place that He promised to prepare for us, to live with Him forever. The shore we should look for is that of the New Earth. If we can see through the fog and picture our eternal home in our mind's eye, it will comfort and energize us.

If you're weary and don't know how you can keep going, I pray this book will give you vision, encouragement, and hope. No matter how tough life gets, if you can see the shore, you'll make it.

I pray this study will help you see the shore.

What practical impact might an excitement about and longing for Heaven have on your Christian life?

_____

_____

_____

_____

What would you like to get from this study?

_____

_____

_____

_____

Take time to pray that God will give you true expectations of Heaven.

DAY 2

Is Heaven Beyond Our Imagination?

OUR TERMINAL DISEASE

As humans we have a terminal disease called mortality. The death rate is 100 percent. Unless Christ returns soon, we're all going to die.

Ancient merchants often wrote the words *memento mori*—"think of death"—in large letters on the first page of their accounting books.[3] Philip of Macedon, father of Alexander the Great, commissioned a servant to stand in his presence each day and say, "Philip, you will die." In contrast, France's Louis XIV decreed that the word *death* not be uttered in his presence. Most of us are more like Louis than Philip, denying death and avoiding the thought of it except when it's forced on us. We live under the fear of death.

List as many reasons as you can why our culture fears and denies death. Plan to discuss this in your group session.

_____

_____

_____

Jesus came to deliver us from the fear of death, "so that by his death he might destroy him who holds the power of death—that is, the devil—and free those who all their lives were held in slavery by their fear of death" (Heb. 2:14-15). Could it be that our culture's rejection of God relates to its fear and denial of death?

THE IMPORTANCE OF USING OUR IMAGINATION

We cannot anticipate or desire what we cannot imagine. I believe that's why God has given us glimpses of Heaven in the Bible—to fire up our imaginations and kindle a desire for Heaven in our hearts. And that's why Satan will always discourage our imagination—or misdirect it to ethereal notions that violate Scripture. As long as the resurrected universe remains either undesirable or unimaginable, Satan succeeds in sabotaging our love for Heaven.

Exhibit A

The writers of Scripture present Heaven in many ways, including as a garden, a city, and a kingdom. Because gardens, cities, and kingdoms are familiar to us, they afford us a bridge to understanding Heaven. However, many people make the mistake of assuming that these are *merely* analogies with no actual correspondence to the reality of Heaven (which would make them poor analogies).

Scripture makes it clear that Jesus is preparing a place for us, and God's kingdom will come to earth. A physical resurrection awaits us. We have no reason to spiritualize or allegorize all earthly descriptions of Heaven. Indeed, some of them may be simple, factual statements. Too often we've been taught that Heaven is a nonphysical realm that cannot have real gardens, cities, kingdoms, buildings, banquets, or bodies. So we fail to take seriously what Scripture tells us about Heaven as a familiar, physical, tangible *place*.

How would you answer the person who insists it is wrong to picture Heaven as a physical place?

_____

_____

Exhibit B

God made us both physical and spiritual. He did not design us to live in a nonphysical realm. We are not, as Plato supposed, merely spiritual beings temporarily encased in bodies. We are physical beings as much as spiritual beings. That's why our bodily resurrection is essential to set us free from sin, the curse, and death forever.

Scripture provides direct and indirect information about the world to come, with enough detail to help us envision it but not so much as to make us think we can completely wrap our minds around it. I believe God expects us to use our imagination, even as we recognize its limitations. If God didn't want us to imagine what Heaven will be like, He wouldn't have told us as much about it.

Rather than ignore our imagination, I believe we should fuel it with Scripture, allowing it to step through the doors that Scripture opens. We should ask God's help to remove the blinders of our preconceived ideas about Heaven so we can understand what the Bible has to say. The Apostle Paul said, "Reflect on what I am saying, for the Lord will give you insight into all this" (2 Tim. 2:7).

How would you feel if you discovered a whole body of clear teaching about Heaven in Scripture that we have missed because of our blinders?

❏ grateful to know I won't be a cloud sitter
❏ upset that I haven't seen this before
❏ other: _____

Everything pleasurable we know about life on earth we have experienced through our senses. So when people portray Heaven as beyond our senses, it alienates and even frightens us. Our misguided attempts to make Heaven sound spiritual merely succeed in making Heaven sound unappealing.

PICTURING HEAVEN

To get a picture of Heaven—which will one day be centered on the New Earth—you don't need to look up at the clouds; you need to look around and imagine this earth without sin, death, suffering, and corruption. I believe Heaven will cause us to gasp in amazement and delight. And that will be just the beginning, because we will not see our real eternal home—the New Earth—until after the resurrection of the dead.

So look out a window. Take a walk. Talk with a friend. Use your God-given skills to paint, draw, build a shed, or write a book. But imagine it—all of it—in its original condition. The happy dog with the wagging tail—not the snarling beast, beaten and starved. The flowers unwilted, the grass undying, the blue sky without pollution. People smiling and joyful—not angry, depressed, and empty. If you're not in a particularly beautiful place, close your eyes and envision the most beautiful place you've ever been—complete with palm trees, raging rivers, jagged mountains, waterfalls, or snow drifts.

Think of friends or family members who loved Jesus and are with Him now. Picture them with you, walking together in this place. All of you have powerful bodies, stronger than those of an Olympic athlete. You are laughing, playing, talking, and reminiscing. You reach up to the tree to pick an apple or orange. You take a bite. It's so sweet it's startling. You've never tasted anything so good. Now you see someone coming toward you. It's Jesus with a big smile on His face. You fall to your knees in worship. He pulls you up and embraces you.

At last you're with the person you were made for, in the place you were made to be. Everywhere you go will have new people and places to enjoy, new things to discover. What's that you smell? A feast. A party's ahead. And you're invited. There's exploration and work to be done—and you can't wait to get started.

Write a prayer expressing to God whatever thoughts, feelings, debates, or ideas the previous paragraphs stirred in you.

I have a biblical basis for all of these statements, and many more. After examining what Scripture says, I hope that next time you hear someone say, "We can't begin to imagine what Heaven will be like," you'll be able to tell them, "I can."

If you were on a debate team, what arguments would you list for why we should use our imagination to picture Heaven?

DAY 3

Is It OK to Imagine Heaven as a Literal Place?

A pastor visiting my office asked what I was writing.

"A big book on Heaven," I said.

"Well," he replied, "since Scripture says 'No eye has seen, no ear has heard, no mind has conceived what God has prepared for those who love him,' what will you be talking about? Obviously, we can't know what God has prepared for us in Heaven." (He was referring to 1 Cor. 2:9.)

Read 1 Corinthians 2:9-10. How would you answer this pastor?

_____

_____

I said, "You didn't complete the sentence. You also have to read verse 10." Here's how the complete sentence reads: "No eye has seen, no ear has heard, no mind has conceived what God has prepared for those who love him—but *God has revealed it to us by his Spirit*" (emphasis added). The context makes clear that this revelation is God's Word (v. 13), which tells us what God has prepared for us.

After reading a few dozen books about Heaven, I came to instinctively cringe whenever I saw 1 Corinthians 2:9. It's a wonderful verse; it's just that it's nearly always misused. It says precisely the opposite of what people cite it to prove! God says He has revealed accurately what we could not know about Heaven. He tells us about Heaven in His Word because He wants us to understand and anticipate what awaits us.

People also pull other verses out to derail discussions about Heaven. For example, "The secret things belong to the Lord our God" (Deut. 29:29). Heaven is regarded as a "secret thing." But the rest of the verse—again, rarely quoted—completes the thought: "But the things revealed belong to us and to our children forever."

We should accept that many things about Heaven are secret and that God has countless surprises in store for us. But God has revealed things to us about Heaven, and they belong to us and to our children. It's critically important that we study and understand them. That is precisely why God revealed them to us!

Have you ever been misquoted as saying something different or even opposite to what you intended? ❏ yes ❏ no

If so, how did you feel?

_____

_____

Another "silencer" is 2 Corinthians 12:2-4 where Paul said he was "caught up to paradise," where he "heard inexpressible things, things that man is not permitted to tell." Some people use this verse to say we should not discuss what Heaven will be like, but it says God didn't permit Paul to talk about his visit to Heaven. In contrast, God commanded John to tell about his visit in the Book of Revelation.

Although it's inappropriate to speculate on what Paul might have seen in Heaven, it's certainly appropriate to discuss what John saw, because God chose to reveal it to us. If He didn't intend for us to under-stand it, why would He bother telling us? (When was the last time you wrote someone a letter using words you didn't expect the person to comprehend?) We should study, teach, and discuss God's revelation about Heaven given to us in His Word.

Isaiah 55:9 is also cited in support of a don't ask, don't tell approach to Heaven: "As the heavens are higher than the earth, so are my ways higher than your ways and my thoughts than your thoughts."

Does this verse in any way imply that we are not to think about Heaven? ❏ yes ❏ no
Why or why not?

_____

_____

God's thoughts are indeed higher than ours, but when He reveals them in Scripture, He expects us to study them, meditate on them, and understand them—again, not exhaustively, but accurately.

SETTING OUR HEARTS
AND MINDS ON HEAVEN

God commands us to set our hearts and minds on Heaven. "Set your hearts on things above, where Christ is seated at the right hand of God" (Col. 3:1). To make sure we don't miss the importance of a heaven-centered life, the next verse says, "Set your minds on things above, not on earthly things."

To long for Christ is to long for Heaven where we will be with Him. God's people are "longing for a better country" (Heb. 11:16). We cannot set our eyes on Christ without setting our eyes on Heaven, and we cannot set our eyes on Heaven without setting our eyes on Christ. Still, it is not only Christ but "things above" we are to set our minds on.

Why do you think God orders us to think deeply about Heaven?

_____

_____

The command and its restatement imply nothing is automatic about setting our minds on Heaven. In fact, most commands assume a resistance to obeying them. The command to think about Heaven is under attack in a hundred different ways every day. Everything works against it. Our minds are so much set on Earth that we are unaccustomed to heavenly thinking. So we must work at it.

What have you been doing daily to set your mind on things above, to seek Heaven?

_____

_____

What should you do differently?

_____

Perhaps you're afraid of becoming "so heavenly minded you're of no earthly good." Relax—you have nothing to worry about! On the contrary, many of us are so earthly minded we are of no heavenly *or* earthly good. C. S. Lewis observed, "If you read history, you will find that the Christians who did most for the present world were just those who thought most of the next. The Apostles themselves, who set on foot the conversion of the Roman Empire, the great men who built up the Middle Ages, the English Evangelicals who abolished the Slave Trade, all left their mark on Earth, precisely because their minds were occupied with Heaven. It is since Christians have largely ceased to think of the other world that they have become so ineffective in this. Aim at Heaven and you will get earth 'thrown in': aim at earth and you will get neither."[4]

We need a generation of heavenly minded people who see human beings and the earth itself not simply as they are, but as God intends for them to be.

FUELING OUR IMAGINATION

We must begin by seeing what Scripture actually says. As a novelist, I take the revelation of God's Word and add to it the vital ingredient of imagination. As C. S. Lewis said, "While reason is the natural organ of truth, imagination is the organ of meaning."[5] And in the words of Francis Schaeffer, "The Christian is the really free man—he is free to have imagination. This too is our heritage. The Christian is the one whose imagination should fly beyond the stars."[6]

Schaeffer always started with God's revealed truth. But he exhorted us to let that truth fuel our imagination. Imagination should not fly away from the truth, but fly upon the truth.

If you're a Christian suffering with great pains and losses, Jesus said, "Be of good cheer" (John 16:33, NKJV). The new house is nearly ready for you. Moving day's coming. The dark winter is about to be transformed into spring. One day soon you will be home—for the first time. Until then, I encourage you to meditate on the Bible's truths about Heaven. May your imagination soar and your heart rejoice.

DAY 4

Is Heaven Our Default Destination?

Unless our sin problem is resolved, the only place we will go is our true default destination —hell.

For every American who believes he's going to hell, 120 believe they're going to Heaven. Contrast this optimism to Christ's words: "Enter through the narrow gate. For wide is the gate and broad is the road that leads to destruction, and many enter through it. But small is the gate and narrow the road that leads to life, and only a few find it" (Matt. 7:13-14).

We all have what would keep us out of Heaven: "All have sinned and fall short of the glory of God" (Rom. 3:23). Sin separates us from a relationship with God (see Isa. 59:2). God is so holy that He cannot allow sin in His presence: "Your eyes are too pure to look on evil; you cannot tolerate wrong" (Hab. 1:13). Because we are sinners, we are not entitled to enter God's presence. We cannot enter Heaven as we are. Heaven is not our default destination. No one goes there automatically. Unless our sin problem is resolved, the only place we will go is our true default destination—hell.

I address this issue now because throughout our study I will talk about being with Jesus in Heaven, being reunited with family and friends, and enjoying great adventures in Heaven. The great danger is that readers will assume they are headed for Heaven. But Jesus made it clear that most people are not going to Heaven: "Small is the gate and narrow the road that leads to life, and only a few find it" (Matt. 7:14).

We dare not "wait and see" when it comes to what's on the other side of death. We can't just cross our fingers and hope our names are written in the book of life (see Rev. 21:27). We can know, we should know, before we die. And because we may die at any time, we need to know now.

The voice that whispers, "There's no hurry. Put this book down; you can always think about it later," is not God's voice. He says, "Now is the day of salvation" (2 Cor. 6:2) and "Choose for yourselves this day whom you will serve" (Josh. 24:15).

Are you certain that you are going to Heaven rather than hell?

❏ yes ❏ no ❏ I'm not sure.

What reason would you give God to admit you to Heaven?

_____

HELL: HEAVEN'S AWFUL ALTERNATIVE

Hell is a place of punishment designed for Satan and the fallen angels (see Matt. 25:41-46; Rev. 20:10). However, it will also be inhabited by people who have rejected God's gift of redemption in Christ (see Rev. 20:12-15). After Christ returns, believers will be resurrected for eternal life in Heaven, and unbelievers will be resurrected for eternal existence in hell (see John 5:28-29). Everyone whose name is not written in the Lamb's book of life will be judged by God according to the works they have done (see Rev. 20:12-15). People without Christ cannot enter the presence of a holy and just God. They will be consigned to a place of everlasting destruction (see Matt. 13:40-42).

Hell will be a place of fire, darkness, weeping, and gnashing of teeth (see Matt. 8:12; 13:42,50; 22:13; 24:51; 25:30; Luke 13:28). It will be a place of conscious punishment for sins, with no hope of relief.

The reality of hell should break our hearts and take us to our knees and to the doors of those without Christ. Today, however, even among many Bible believers, hell has become "the h word," seldom named, rarely talked about. It's common to deny or ignore the clear teaching of Scripture about hell. Hell seems disproportionate, a divine overreaction.

Many think it civilized, humane, and compassionate to deny the existence of an eternal hell. In fact it is arrogant that we, as creatures, would dare to take what we think is the moral high ground against what God has clearly revealed. We don't want to believe that anybody deserves eternal punishment because if they do, so do we. But if we understood God's nature and ours, we would be shocked not that some people could go to hell (where else would sinners go?), but that any would be permitted into Heaven. By denying the endlessness of hell, we minimize Christ's work on the cross, because we lower the stakes of redemption. If Christ's crucifixion and resurrection didn't deliver us

We should be shocked not that some people could go to hell, but that any would be permitted into Heaven.

from an eternal hell, His work on the cross is less heroic, less potent, less consequential, and thus less deserving of our praise.

Mark these statements *True* or *False* according to the preceding paragraph.

___ We are more compassionate when we deny hell.

___ When we deny hell, we set ourselves above God as morally superior.

___ Denying the existence of hell honors God's nature.

___ If we admit anyone deserves hell, we convict ourselves.

Satan has obvious motives for fueling our denial of eternal punishment. He wants unbelievers to reject Christ without fear; he wants Christians to be unmotivated to share Christ; and he wants God to receive less glory for the radical nature of Christ's redemptive work.

WHAT DID JESUS SAY ABOUT HELL?

Many books deny hell. Some embrace the belief that all people will ultimately be saved. Some consider hell the invention of wild-eyed prophets obsessed with wrath. They argue that Christians should take the higher road of Christ's love. But this perspective overlooks a conspicuous reality: In the Bible, Jesus said more about hell than anyone else (see Matt. 10:28; 13:40-42; Mark 9:43-44). He referred to it as a literal place and described it in graphic terms—including raging fires, darkness, teeth gnashing, and the worm that doesn't die.

In Jesus' story of the rich man and Lazarus, He taught that in hell the wicked suffer terribly; are fully conscious; retain their desires, memories, and reasoning; long for relief; cannot be comforted; cannot leave their torment; and are bereft of hope (see Luke 16:19-31). The Savior could not have painted a more bleak or graphic picture.

How long will hell last? "They will go away to eternal punishment," Jesus said of the unrighteous, "but the righteous to eternal life" (Matt. 25:46). Here, in the same sentence, Christ uses the same word translated "eternal" *(aionos)* to describe the duration of *both* Heaven and hell.

Thus, if Heaven will be consciously experienced forever, hell *must* be consciously experienced forever.

C. S. Lewis said, "I have met no people who fully disbelieved in Hell and also had a living- and life-giving belief in Heaven." The biblical teaching stands or falls together on both destinations.

If I had a choice, that is, if Scripture were not so clear and conclusive, I would certainly not believe in hell. Trust me when I say I do not *want* to believe in it. But if I make what I want—or what others want—the basis for my beliefs, then I am a follower of myself and my culture, not a follower of Christ. "There seems to be a kind of conspiracy," writes novelist Dorothy Sayers, "to forget, or to conceal, where the doctrine of hell comes from. The doctrine of hell is not 'mediaeval priestcraft' for frightening people into giving money to the church: it is Christ's deliberate judgment on sin. ... We cannot repudiate Hell without altogether repudiating Christ."[7]

IS IT UNLOVING TO SPEAK OF HELL?

If you were giving some friends directions to Denver and you knew that one road led there but a second road ended at a sharp cliff around a blind corner, would you talk only about the safe road? No. You would tell them about both, especially if you knew that the road to destruction was wider and more traveled. In fact, it would be terribly unloving not to warn them about that other road.

For the same reason, we must not believe Satan's lie that it's unloving to speak to people about hell. The most basic truth is only two possible destinations after death exist: Heaven and hell. Each is just as real and just as eternal as the other. Unless and until we surrender our lives to Jesus Christ, we're headed for hell. The most loving thing we can do for our friends and our family is to warn them about the road that leads to destruction and tell them about the road that leads to life.

It would upset us, but would we think it unloving if a doctor told us we had a potentially fatal cancer? And would the doctor not tell us if the cancer could be eradicated? Why then do we not tell unsaved people about the cancer of sin and evil and how the inevitable penalty of eternal destruction can be avoided by Jesus Christ's atoning sacrifice?

How would you answer that last question? (Plan to discuss it with your group.)

_____

_____

_____

EARTH: THE IN-BETWEEN WORLD

God and Satan are not equal opposites. Likewise, hell is not Heaven's equal opposite. Just as God has no equal as a person, Heaven has no equal as a place.

Hell will be agonizingly dull, small, and insignificant; without company, camaraderie, purpose, or accomplishment. It will not have its own stories; it will merely be a footnote on history, a crack in the pavement. As the new universe moves gloriously onward, hell and its occupants will exist in utter inactivity and insignificance, an eternal nonlife of regret and—perhaps—diminishing personhood.

Scripture says of those who die without Jesus, "They will be punished with everlasting destruction and shut out from the presence of the Lord and from the majesty of his power" (2 Thess. 1:9). Because God is the source of all good and hell is the absence of God, hell must also be the absence of all good. Hell will have no community, no camaraderie, no friendship. I don't believe hell is a place where demons take delight in punishing people and where people commiserate over their fate. More likely, each person is in solitary confinement, just as the rich man is portrayed alone in hell (see Luke 16:22-23). Misery loves company, but there will be nothing to love in hell.

Earth is an in-between world touched by both Heaven and hell. Earth leads directly into Heaven or directly into hell, affording a choice between the two. The best of life on Earth is a glimpse of Heaven; the worst of life is a glimpse of hell. For Christians, this present life is the closest they will come to hell. For unbelievers, it is the closest they will come to Heaven.

The reality of the choice that lies before us in this life is both wonderful and awful. Given the reality of our two possible destinations, shouldn't we be willing to pay any price to avoid hell and go to Heaven? And yet, the price has already been paid. "You were bought at a price" (1 Cor. 6:20). The price paid was exorbitant—the shed blood of God Himself.

Consider the wonder of it: God determined that He would rather suffer torment on our behalf than live in Heaven without us. He so much wants us not to go to hell that He paid a horrible price on the cross so that we wouldn't have to.

As it stands, however, apart from Christ, our eternal future will be spent in hell.

What aspect of hell do you find most troubling?

_____

_____

_____

The price has been paid; our lives have been ransomed. But still we must choose. Like any gift, forgiveness can be offered, but it isn't ours until we choose to receive it. Christ offers each of us the gift of forgiveness and eternal life—but just because the offer is made doesn't make it ours. To have it, we must choose to accept it.

DAY 5

Can You Know You're Going to Heaven?

Ancient cities kept rolls of their citizens. Guards were posted at the city gates to keep out criminals and enemies by checking their names against the list. This is the context for Revelation 21:27: "Nothing impure will ever enter [the city], nor will anyone who does what is shameful or deceitful, but only those whose names are written in the Lamb's book of life."

Ruthanna Metzgar, a professional singer, tells a story that illustrates the importance of having our names written in the book. Several years ago she was asked to sing at the wedding of a very wealthy man. She and her husband, Roy, were very excited about attending.

After the wedding, waiters in tuxedos offered luscious hors d'oeuvres and exotic beverages. The bride and groom approached a beautiful glass and brass staircase that led to the top floor. Someone ceremoniously cut a satin ribbon draped across the bottom of the stairs. They announced the wedding feast was about to begin. Bride and groom ascended the stairs, followed by their guests.

At the top of the stairs, a maitre d' with a bound book greeted the guests outside the doors.

"May I have your name please?"

"I am Ruthanna Metzgar and this is my husband, Roy."

He searched the *M's*. "I'm not finding it. Would you spell it please?"

Ruthanna spelled her name slowly. After searching the book, the maitre d' looked up and said, "I'm sorry, but your name isn't here."

"There must be some mistake," Ruthanna replied. "I'm the singer. I sang for this wedding!"

The gentleman answered, "It doesn't matter who you are or what you did. Without your name in the book you cannot attend the banquet."

He motioned to a waiter and said, "Show these people to the service elevator, please."

The Metzgars followed the waiter past beautifully decorated tables laden with shrimp, whole smoked salmon, and magnificent carved ice sculptures. Adjacent to the banquet area, an orchestra was preparing to perform, all dressed in dazzling white tuxedos.

The waiter led Ruthanna and Roy to the service elevator, ushered them in, and pushed *G* for the parking garage.

After locating their car and driving several miles in silence, Roy reached over and put his hand on Ruthanna's arm. "Sweetheart, what happened?"

"When the invitation arrived, I was busy," Ruthanna replied. "I never bothered to RSVP. Besides, I was the singer. Surely I could go to the reception without returning the RSVP!"

Ruthanna started to weep—not only because she had missed the most lavish banquet she'd ever been invited to, but also because she suddenly had a small taste of what it will be like someday for people as they stand before Christ and find their names are not written in the Lamb's book of life.[8]

Write a moral to the story of Ruthanna's experience.

_____

_____

Throughout the ages, countless people have been too busy to respond to Christ's invitation to His wedding banquet. Many assume that the good they've done—perhaps attending church, being baptized, singing in the choir, or helping in a soup kitchen—will be enough to gain entry to Heaven. But people who do not respond to Christ's invitation to forgive their sins are people whose names aren't written in the Lamb's book of life. To be denied entrance to Heaven's wedding banquet will not just mean going down the service elevator to the garage. It will mean being cast outside into hell, forever.

In that day, no explanation or excuse will count. All that will matter is whether our names are written in the book. If they're not, we'll be turned away.

Have you said yes to Christ's invitation to join Him at the wedding feast and spend eternity with Him in His house? If so, you have reason to rejoice—Heaven's gates will be open to you.

If you have been putting off your response, your RSVP, or if you presume that you can enter Heaven without responding to Christ's invitation, one day you will deeply regret it.

Look to the question on page 21 about the reason you should give to be allowed into Heaven. Was it more nearly:
- ❏ because I've been good
- ❏ because I've RSVP'd to God's invitation
- ❏ because everybody deserves entry to Heaven

Can we really know in advance where we're going when we die? The Apostle John, who wrote about the New Heaven and New Earth, said, "I write these things to you who believe in the name of the Son of God so that *you may know that you have eternal life*" (1 John 5:13, emphasis added). We *can* know for sure that we have eternal life. We can know for sure that we will go to Heaven when we die.

Do you?

People who want to get to Florida don't simply get in the car and start driving, hoping the road will somehow get them there. Instead, they look at a map and chart their course. They do this in advance rather than waiting until they arrive at the wrong destination or discover they've spent three days driving the wrong direction. If you want to get somewhere, guesswork is a poor strategy. The goal of getting to Heaven is worthy of greater advanced planning than we would give to any other journey—yet some people spend far more time preparing for a trip to Disney World.

WHAT YOU NEED TO KNOW AND DO

Because of Jesus Christ's sacrificial death on the cross on our behalf, God freely offers us forgiveness. "He does not treat us as our sins deserve or repay us according to our iniquities. ... As far as the east is from the west, so far has he removed our transgressions from us" (Ps. 103:10,12).

Forgiveness is not automatic. If we want to be forgiven, we must recognize and repent of our sins: "He who conceals his sins does not prosper, but whoever confesses and renounces them finds mercy" (Prov. 28:13). We establish forgiveness by our confession: "If we confess our sins, he is faithful and just and will forgive us our sins and purify us from all unrighteousness" (1 John 1:9).

Christ offers to everyone the gift of forgiveness, salvation, and eternal life: "Whoever is thirsty, let him come; and whoever wishes, let him take the free gift of the water of life" (Rev. 22:17).

No righteous deed we can do will earn us a place in Heaven (Titus 3:5). We come to Christ empty-handed. We can take no credit for salvation: "For it is by grace you have been saved, through faith—and this not from yourselves, it is the gift of God—not by works, so that no one can boast" (Eph. 2:8-9).

We cannot work for, earn, or achieve this gift. It does not depend on our merit or effort but solely on Christ's generous and sufficient sacrifice on our behalf. Ultimately, God's greatest gift is Himself. We don't just need salvation; we need Jesus the Savior. It is the person, God, who graciously gives us the place, Heaven.

Do not merely assume that you are a Christian and are going to Heaven. Make the conscious decision to accept Christ's sacrificial death on your behalf. When you choose to accept Christ and surrender control of your life to Him, you can be certain that your name will be written in the Lamb's book of life.

Check each of the following you have done:

❑ I have confessed my sins.

❑ I have asked Christ to forgive me.

❑ I placed my trust in Christ's death and resurrection on my behalf.

❑ I asked Jesus to be my Lord and empower me to follow Him.

A good church will teach truth and provide love, help, and support. If you have further questions about Jesus and about Heaven, you can find answers there.

WATER FOR THE THIRSTY

For those who know Christ, their place is Heaven. For those who do not know Christ, their place is hell. Jesus said, "I am the way and the truth and the life. No one comes to the Father except through me" (John 14:6). There is no middle ground. Either you are a follower of Jesus or you are not. Christ said, "He who is not with me is against me" (Luke 11:23).

The Bible ends with yet one more invitation, suggesting that God wants to give every reader one last chance: "The Spirit and the bride say, 'Come!' And let him who hears say, 'Come!' Whoever is thirsty, let him come; and whoever wishes, let him take the free gift of the water of life" (Rev. 22:17). It is Jesus—and Heaven—we thirst for. Jesus and Heaven are offered to us at no cost because He already paid the price for us.

"Seek the LORD while he may be found; call on him while he is near." ISAIAH 55:6

God invites you to come. The church invites you to come. As a follower of Jesus, I invite you to come.

You are made for a person and a place. Jesus is the person. Heaven is the place. They are a package—you cannot get Heaven without Jesus or Jesus without Heaven.

Wouldn't it be tragic if you read this study on Heaven and then didn't get to go there?

If you aren't certain you'd be allowed into Heaven, would you write a prayer responding to God's invitation? Be sure to include these elements:

1. Admission of sin

_____

_____

_____

2. Acceptance of Christ's completed work

_____

_____

_____

3. Surrender to Jesus as Savior and Lord

_____

_____

_____

1. Barry Morrow, *Heaven Observed* (Colorado Springs: Nav Press, 2001), 89,
2. C. J. Mahaney, "Loving the Church" (taped message, Covenant Life Church, Gaithersburg, MD, n.d.).
3. Basilea Schlink, *What Comes After Death?* (Carol Stream, IL: Creation House, 1976), 20.
4. C. S. Lewis, *Mere Christianity* (New York: Collier, 1960), 118.
5. C. S. Lewis, "Bluespels and Flalanspheres: A Semantic Nightmare," quoted in Walter Hooper, ed., *Selected Literary Essays* (Cambridge: Cambridge University Press, 1969).
6. Francis Schaeffer, *Art and the Bible* (Downers Grove, IL: InterVarsity, 1973), 61.
7. Dorothy Sayers, *A Matter of Eternity,* ed. Rosamond Kent Sprague (Grand Rapids, MI: Eerdmans, 1973), 86.
8. Ruthanna C. Metzgar, from her story "It's Not in the Book!" copyright © 1998 by Ruthanna C. Metzgar. Used by permission. For the full story in Ruthanna's own words, see *www.epm.org/articles/metzgar.html*

Understanding the Present Heaven

DAY 1

What Is the Present Heaven?

Most of this study centers on the eternal Heaven—the place we will live forever after the final resurrection. But because we've all had loved ones who have died and we will also die unless Christ returns first, let us consider what Scripture teaches about the present Heaven—the place Christians go when they die.

At death, the human spirit goes either to God's presence or is separated from Him. When Christ-followers die, they enter what theologians call the intermediate state, a transitional period between our past lives on earth and our future resurrection to life on the New earth. When we tell our children "Grandma's now in Heaven," we're referring to the present Heaven.

Scripture says, "The dust returns to the ground it came from, and the spirit returns to God who gave it" (Eccl. 12:7). The Apostle Paul said that to die was to be with Christ (see Phil. 1:23) and to be absent from the body was to be present with the Lord (2 Cor. 5:8). These passages make clear no "soul sleep" exists between life on earth and life in Heaven. The phrase "fallen asleep" (see 1 Thess. 4:13 and similar passages) is a euphemism for death, describing the body's outward appearance. The spirit's departure from the body ends our earthly existence. The physical part of us "sleeps" until the resurrection, while the spiritual part of us relocates to a conscious existence in Heaven (Dan. 12:2-3; 2 Cor. 5:8).

Have you understood the Bible to teach the present Heaven?

❑ Yes, I assumed everybody knows this.

❑ No, it's new to me.

❑ I never thought about it this way.

❑ I'm still not sure. Convince me.

What excites, interests, or confuses you about this teaching?

_____

_____

WILL WE LIVE IN HEAVEN FOREVER?

In the present Heaven, we'll be joyfully in Christ's presence but looking forward to our bodily resurrection and permanent relocation to the New Earth. Though a wonderful place, the present Heaven is not the place God promises for us to live forever. God's children are destined for life as resurrected beings on a resurrected earth.

It may seem strange that the Heaven we go to at death isn't eternal, yet it's true. "Christians often talk about living with God 'in heaven' forever," writes theologian Wayne Grudem. "But in fact the biblical teaching is richer than that: it tells us that there will be new heavens and a new earth—an entirely renewed creation—and we will live with God there ... There will be a joining of heaven and earth in this new creation."[1]

Let me suggest an analogy to illustrate the difference between the present and eternal Heaven. Suppose you lived in a homeless shelter in Miami. One day you inherit a beautiful house, fully furnished, on a gorgeous hillside overlooking Santa Barbara, California. With the home comes a wonderful job doing what you've always wanted, and you'll also be near family members who moved from Miami many years ago.

On your flight to Santa Barbara, you'll change planes in Dallas, where you'll spend an afternoon. Some other family members, whom you haven't seen in years, will meet you at the Dallas airport and board the plane with you to Santa Barbara. You look forward to seeing them.

Now, when the Miami ticket agent asks you, "Where are you headed?" would you say "Dallas"? No. You would say Santa Barbara, because that's your final destination. If you mentioned Dallas at all, you would only say, "I'm going to Santa Barbara by way of Dallas."

When you talk to your friends in Miami you might not even mention Dallas, even though you will be a Dallas-dweller for several hours. Even if you spent a week in Dallas, it wouldn't be your focus. Your true destination—your new permanent home—would be Santa Barbara. Similarly, the Heaven we will go to when we die, the present Heaven, is a temporary dwelling place, a stop along the way to our final destination: the New Earth.

Label the appropriate cities "Earth," "Present Heaven," and "Heaven" according to my analogy.

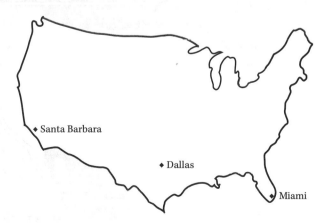

A more precise analogy would be leaving the homeless shelter in Miami, flying to Dallas, and then turning around and going back home to your place of origin, which has been completely renovated—a new Miami. In this new Miami you would no longer live in a homeless shelter but in a beautiful house in a glorious pollution-free, crime-free, sin-free city. So you would end up living not in a new home but a radically improved version of your old home. This is what the Bible promises us—we will live with Christ and each other forever, not in the present Heaven, but on the New Earth, where God will be at home with His people.

DOES HEAVEN REALLY CHANGE?

From experience, I can hear some people turning pages in their Bibles looking for Hebrews 13:8.

Why might some people use that passage to argue against the idea of the present Heaven? _____

_____

What does the passage actually say never changes?
❑ Heaven   ❑ The Church   ❑ Jesus Christ

God created Heaven not as a place He *must* dwell but where He *chooses* to dwell. Because God created Heaven, it had a beginning and is therefore neither timeless nor changeless. It had a past (the time prior to Christ's incarnation, death, and resurrection), it has a present (the present Heaven, where believers go when they die), and it will have a future (the eternal Heaven, or New Earth). The past Heaven, the present Heaven, and the eternal Heaven can all be called Heaven, yet they are not synonymous.

Books on Heaven often fail to distinguish between the present and eternal states, using the one word—Heaven—as all-inclusive. But this has dulled our thinking and keeps us from understanding important biblical distinctions. In this study, when referring to the place believers go after death, I use terms such as the present Heaven or the intermediate Heaven. I'll refer to the eternal state as the eternal Heaven or the New Earth. I hope you can see why this is such an important distinction. The present Heaven is a waiting place until the return of Christ and our bodily resurrection. The eternal Heaven, the New Earth, is our true home where we will live forever with our Lord and each other. The great redemptive promises of God will find their ultimate fulfillment on the New Earth, not in the present Heaven.

How would you explain each of the different states of Heaven?

1. The past Heaven

_____

_____

2. The present Heaven

_____

_____

3. The eternal Heaven

_____

_____

Much of what we say about the eternal Heaven may not be true of the present Heaven. (For instance, we will eat and drink in our resurrection bodies on the New Earth, but that doesn't necessarily mean we will eat and drink in the present Heaven.) And when we describe the present Heaven, it will not necessarily correspond with what the eternal Heaven, the New Earth, will be like. Once we abandon our assumption that Heaven cannot change, it all makes sense. God does not change, but God clearly says that Heaven will. It will eventually be relocated to the New Earth (Rev. 21:1).

Does anything we've studied today change your thinking?
❏ yes ❏ no **If so, explain.**

_____

_____

> Much of what we say about the eternal Heaven may not be true of the present Heaven.

I completed the assignment by sharing with _____ (initials) on _____ (date).

DAY 2

What Is the Significance of the Future Heaven?

What is Heaven like? and *What will Heaven be like?* have different answers. The present Heaven is in the angelic realm, separate from earth. By contrast, the future Heaven will be in the human realm, on earth. The dwelling place of God will be the dwelling place of humanity, in a resurrected universe (see Rev. 21:1-3 in margin). Heaven, God's dwelling place, will one day be on the New Earth.

That God would come down to the New Earth to live with us fits perfectly with His original plan. God could have taken Adam and Eve up to Heaven to visit with Him in His world. Instead, He came down to walk with them in theirs (Gen. 3:8). God's ultimate plan was not to take us up to live in a realm made for Him but to come down and live with us in the realm He made for us.

The next paragraph summarizes God's entire plan. Ask someone to discuss it with you as a class assignment. Mark the margin when you complete the assignment.

In Genesis 1–3, we see that earth was Heaven's backyard. There was nothing about a physical realm that God found unappealing or incompatible with Himself. On the contrary, He created the physical universe as an act of self-expression. He handcrafted both man and earth in anticipation of His becoming man and living on earth. The incarnation was no afterthought—as He created man's body from earth, God the Son knew He would one day have such a body and live on earth. He came to dwell with fallen men on the cursed earth so He might purchase back both man and earth and spend eternity with redeemed mankind on a redeemed earth. As the preincarnate Christ walked and talked with the first man and woman in Eden, so He will walk and talk with all redeemed men and women on the New Earth.

We have a clear reference point to understand the eternal Heaven. Eden, an earth untouched by sin, is that reference point. We should view Eden as Heaven's template, a blueprint for the New Earth. As Jesus is God incarnate, so the New Earth will be Heaven incarnate.

WHAT IS THE SIGNIFICANCE OF THE NEW JERUSALEM?

The present incompatibility between Heaven and earth is temporary—Earth is under sin and the curse. Once that is fixed, Heaven and earth will be fully compatible again (see Eph. 1:9-10). Scripture highlights the future connection by the New Jerusalem "coming down" from Heaven.

The city's exact dimensions are reported to measure the equivalent of 1,400 miles (Rev. 21:15-17). While these proportions may have symbolic importance, this doesn't mean they can't be literal. Scripture emphasizes they are in "man's measurement" (Rev. 21:17). A metropolis of this size would stretch from Canada to Mexico and from the Appalachian Mountains to the California border. We don't need to worry that Heaven will be crowded. The ground level of the city will be over 2,000,000 square miles.

The New Jerusalem will be different from any city we've ever known—it will have all the advantages we associate with earthly cities but none of the disadvantages. The city will be filled with natural wonders, magnificent architecture, thriving culture, and no crime, pollution, garbage, or homelessness. It will truly be Heaven on earth. Imagine moving through the city to enjoy arts, music, and sports without pickpockets, porn shops, drugs, or prostitution. Imagine sitting down to eat and raising glasses to toast the King, who will be glorified in every pleasure we enjoy.

Which activities do you most anticipate? Think in these areas:

physical _____

cultural _____

learning_____

hobbies _____

"He made known to us the mystery of His will ... to bring all things in heaven and on earth together under one head, even Christ."

EPHESIANS 1:9,10

Heaven knows no elitism; because of Christ's blood everyone will have access to the city's parks, museums, restaurants, libraries, concerts—anything and everything it has to offer. Nobody will have to peek over the fence or look longingly through the windows.

How does sharing with a friend an activity you enjoy enhance your joy? _____

_____

The Artist's fingerprints will be seen everywhere in the great city. Every feature will speak of His attributes. The priceless stones will speak of His beauty and grandeur. The open gates will speak of His accessibility. All who wish to come to Him at His throne may do so at any time. God will delight to share with us the glories of His capital city ... and ours.

WHAT'S THE RIVER OF LIFE?

On the New Earth, we won't have to leave the city to find natural beauty. John described a natural wonder in the center of the New Jerusalem: "the river of the water of life, as clear as crystal, flowing from the throne of God and of the Lamb down the middle of the great street of the city" (Rev. 22:1-2). Can you picture people talking and laughing beside this river? This fully accessible natural wonder on the city's main street is amazing—something that would be featured in any travel brochure.

What is your favorite river or body of water on the present earth?

_____

What special meaning or memories does this body of water hold for you? _____

_____

_____

The city has many other streets, of course, but none like this, for this one leads directly to the King's throne. The fact that the water is flowing down from it suggests the throne's high elevation. One need only follow the street—or the river—up to its source, to arrive at the city's center-piece: the Lamb's throne.

WHAT'S THE TREE OF LIFE?

After John described the river of life, he mentioned another striking feature: "On each side of the river stood the tree of life, bearing twelve crops of fruit, yielding its fruit every month. And the leaves of the tree are for the healing of the nations" (Rev. 22:2).

What memories from your childhood deal with trees?

❏ climbing them ❏ eating fruit from them
❏ sitting in the shade of them ❏ other _____

Describe one memory: _____
_____

Why do you suppose God chose a tree or trees to convey life to His children? (no correct answer, just share your thoughts)
_____
_____

In Eden, the tree appears to have been a source of ongoing physical life. Instead of a natural human immortality, the presence of the tree of life suggests a supernatural provision through people eating. In the New Earth we will eat freely the fruit of the same tree that nourished Adam and Eve: "To him who overcomes, I will give the right to eat from the tree of life, which is in the paradise of God" (Rev. 2:7). Once more human beings will draw their strength and vitality through eating of this tree.

Perfectly healthy people needing food, water and health-giving vegetation on the New Earth signals no inconsistency—as long as it's readily available. We'll apparently not be without needs, but all our needs will be met.

Which would you choose?

❏ To have no needs ❏ To have all your needs met

How would you answer the question posed by today's title: *What is the significance of the future heaven?* _____

_____

_____

What has God shown you today that makes you more willing to live sacrificially for Him? _____

_____

_____

D A Y   3

Is the Present Heaven a Physical Place?

After reading one of my books, a missionary wrote to me, deeply troubled that I thought Heaven might be a physical place. No matter how many Scripture passages I pointed to, it didn't matter. He'd always been taught that Heaven was "spiritual" and therefore not physical. To suggest otherwise was, in his mind, to commit heresy.

My concern was not so much that he believed the present Heaven isn't physical. (Maybe he's right.) Rather, it was that he seemed convinced that if Heaven were physical, it would make it less sacred and special. He viewed physical and spiritual as opposites. When I asked him to demonstrate from Scripture why Heaven cannot be a physical place, he told me the answer was very simple: because "God is spirit" (John 4:24). He believed that verse settled the question once and for all.

How would you respond to the missionary's argument?

_____

_____

Saying that God is spirit is very different from saying that Heaven is spirit. Heaven, after all, is not the same as God. God created Heaven.

If we draw inferences about the nature of Heaven, we shouldn't derive them from the nature of God. After all, He is a one-of-a-kind being who is infinite, existing outside of space and time. Rather, we should base our deductions on the nature of humanity. It's no problem for the infinite God to dwell wherever mankind dwells. The question is whether finite humans can exist as God does—outside of space and time. I'm not certain we can (see 2 Cor. 5:2-4). But I am certain that if we can, it is only as a temporary aberration that will be permanently corrected by our bodily resurrection in preparation for life on the New Earth.

In the next three paragraphs, underline clues that suggest why many people have overlooked what the Bible says about Heaven.

Why are we so resistant to the idea that Heaven could be physical? The answer, I believe, comes from an unbiblical belief that the spirit realm is good and the material world is bad. I call this view christoplatonism.

Plato, the Greek philosopher, believed that material things, including the human body and the earth, are evil, while immaterial things such as the soul and Heaven are good. This view is called Platonism. The Christian church, highly influenced by Platonism, came to embrace the view that human spirits are better off without bodies and that Heaven is a disembodied state. They rejected the notion of Heaven as a physical realm and spiritualized or entirely neglected the biblical teaching of resurrected people inhabiting a resurrected earth.

Platonism had a devastating effect on our ability to understand what Scripture says about Heaven, particularly about the eternal Heaven, the New Earth. A fine Christian man said to me, "This idea of having bodies and eating food and being in an earthly place—it just sounds so unspiritual." If we believe, even subconsciously, that bodies and the earth and material things are unspiritual, even evil, then we will inevitably reject or spiritualize any biblical revelation about our bodily resurrection or the physical characteristics of the New Earth. That's exactly what has happened in most Christian churches, and it's a large reason for our failure to come to terms with a biblical doctrine of Heaven.

Write either *True* or *False* by each of the following statements about christoplatonism.

____ It is based on an unbiblical belief that the spirit realm is good and the material world is bad.

____ It embraces the view that human spirits are better off without bodies.

____ It leads to an appreciation of the resurrection and Heaven.

____ It is responsible for our failure to see many things the Bible says about Heaven.

Write your own definition of christoplatonism.

_____

_____

You could describe christoplatonism a variety of ways. I hope your definition includes the idea that the physical world is evil and the world of spirit is good. You get extra credit if you added that christoplatonists believe heaven is an immaterial spirit realm.

HEAVEN AS SUBSTANCE, EARTH AS SHADOW

God's word to Moses in Hebrews 8:5 suggests the intriguing idea of earth as Heaven's shadow. Several Scriptures suggest we should see earth as a derivative realm and Heaven as the source realm (see Rev. 7:9; 8:6,13; 19:14). We should stop thinking of Heaven and earth as opposites and view them as overlapping circles that share certain commonalities.

What sights or events on earth cause you to think of Heaven?

_____

_____

How does the idea that those elements reflect items in Heaven impact your thinking? _____

_____

_____

"These serve as a copy and shadow of the heavenly things, as Moses was warned when he was about to complete the tabernacle. For He said, 'Be careful that you make everything according to the pattern that was shown to you on the mountain.'"

HEBREWS 8:5

How does Romans 1:20 support the idea of earth as the derivative of Heaven? _____

_____

Why do you suppose many Christians automatically assume all references to Heaven are nonphysical? _____

_____

If you responded *christoplatonism*, I think you are right on target. God created earth in the image of Heaven, just as He created mankind in His image. C. S. Lewis proposed that "the hills and valleys of Heaven will be to those you now experience not as a copy is to an original, nor as a substitute is to the genuine article, but as the flower to the root, or the diamond to the coal."[2]

We often think backward. We tend to start with earth and reason up toward Heaven, when instead we should start with Heaven and reason down toward earth. For instance, when God calls Himself a father and us children, He's not just accommodating Himself to our earthly family structure. On the contrary, He created father-child relationships to display His relationships with us, just as He created human marriage to reveal the love relationship between Christ and His bride (Eph. 5:32).

THE PRESENT HEAVEN
DESCRIBED AS PARADISE

Jesus told the thief on the cross, "Today you will be with me in paradise" (Luke 23:43). He was referring to the present Heaven. The word Jesus used to describe the present Heaven, *paradise,* comes from a Persian word, meaning "a walled park" or "enclosed garden." People do not leave a garden or park to grow entirely on its own. We bring our creativity to bear on managing, cultivating, and presenting it.

How does Genesis 2:8-9,15 combine the elements of wild nature with human orderliness? _____

_____

_____

What kinds of tasks do you think would grow out of Adam and Eve's original job description?

❑ farming and ranching   ❑ homebuilding

❑ exploration   ❑ landscape architecture

❑ criminal justice   ❑ inventing

❑ art teaching   ❑ smuggling

❑ science   ❑ other_____

What occupations would you like to try if you weren't prevented by lack of time or opportunity? (Plan to discuss this with your group.) _____

_____

_____

"He drove man out, and east of the garden of Eden He stationed cherubim with a flaming, whirling sword to guard the way to the tree of life." GENESIS 3:24

After the fall, Eden was not destroyed. Humans lost the ability to live there. Eden appears to have remained just as it was, a physical paradise removed to a realm where we can't go—most likely the present Heaven.

Where does Revelation 2:7 indicate the tree of life is now?

❑ Des Moines   ❑ Paradise   ❑ Heaven

God is not finished with Eden. He preserved it as a place mankind will one day occupy again—and to a certain extent may now occupy in the present Heaven. Because we're told that the tree of life will be located in the New Jerusalem (Rev. 22:2), it seems likely that the original Eden may be a great park at the center of the city. If we know the tree that distinguished Eden will be there, why not Eden itself? This would fit perfectly with the statement in Revelation 2:7 that the tree of life is presently in Paradise. The tree of life's presence in the New Jerusalem establishes that elements of Eden, as physical as the original, will again be part of the human experience.

Go for a walk or look at some pictures of nature. Try to pick out elements that, though we live in a fallen world, still reflect the beauty and design of paradise.

DAY 4

Do People Have Bodies in the Present Heaven?

Given the consistent physical descriptions of the present Heaven and those who dwell there, it seems possible—though certainly debatable—that between our earthly life and our bodily resurrection, God may grant us some physical form while in that unnatural state "between bodies," awaiting our resurrection.

Read Revelation 10:9-10 carefully and answer the following *True* or *False* about John's experience in the present Heaven.

_____ He could grasp and hold things.

_____ He could fly from one place to another.

_____ He could taste and eat things.

_____ He appears to have had a physical body.

Apparently the Apostle John had a body when he visited Heaven. To assume this is figurative language is not a restriction demanded by the text but only by our presupposition that Heaven isn't a physical place. (Only answer 2 is false.) If those in Heaven receive temporary forms—and I recognize it only as a possibility—it would in no way minimize the absolute necessity of our future resurrection, emphatically established in 1 Corinthians 15:12-32. In fact, only on the basis of that future certainty might temporary bodies be given—just as in Old Testament times the certainty of Christ's future death and resurrection permitted people who would otherwise have been hell-bound to enter Paradise.

JESUS IN HEAVEN

The resurrected Christ now dwells in Heaven. On earth His resurrected body was physical, and this same, physical Jesus ascended to Heaven, from which He will one day return to earth (Acts 1:11). It seems indisputable, then, that at least one physical body is in the present Heaven.

If Christ's body in the present Heaven has physical properties, it stands to reason that others in Heaven would have physical forms as well, even if only temporary ones. It also makes sense that other aspects of the present Heaven would have physical properties—so that, for example, when Christ is seen standing at the right hand of God (Acts 7:56), He is actually standing on something. If we know there is physical substance in Heaven (namely, Christ's body), can we not also assume that other references to physical objects in Heaven, including physical forms, are literal rather than figurative?

Enoch and Elijah appear to have been taken to Heaven in their physical bodies too (Gen. 5:24; Heb. 11:5; 2 Kings 2:11-12). We do not know how bodies under the curse could be taken to Heaven, but it appears that they were. Our spirits are also under the curse, but based on Christ's redemptive work they are allowed entrance to Heaven. Perhaps God extended the same grace to allow the bodies of Enoch and Elijah into the present Heaven. The physical presence of Moses and Elijah at the Transfiguration seems to demonstrate beyond question that God at least sometimes creates intermediate bodies for people to inhabit prior to the resurrection of the dead.

I've set out to change some ideas about Heaven, so how am I doing?

I don't believe a word of it.	OK, the Bible says more about the present Heaven than I thought.	You're boring me. I already knew this stuff.

WHAT CAN WE LEARN FROM THE RICH MAN AND LAZARUS?

Some believe the story of the rich man and Lazarus (see Luke 16:19-31) is nothing more than a parable. In it, however, Jesus ascribed physical properties to people who had died. I certainly don't believe every biblical account should be taken literally, and I agree the story contains much figurative language. However, I also think it's a mistake to declare details strictly figurative based on the assumptions of christoplatonism.

Read Luke 16:19-31. What statements seem to indicate Jesus was talking about real people?

_____

_____

Did you know that this is the only parable Jesus told in which He gave a specific name to someone in the story? Naming Lazarus suggests Jesus was speaking of a real man. Furthermore, if Jesus made up the name for the poor man, why would he choose the name of Lazarus—His close friend, who was actually a rich man? Wouldn't using Lazarus's name have inevitably created confusion—two different Lazaruses who die and live again, one in Paradise, the other on earth?

The best explanation for why Jesus called the man Lazarus may be because he was a real man, and that was his name. If so, it increases the probability that Jesus was telling us about what actually happened to two men after they died. It seems unlikely that Jesus would have depicted the afterlife in such detail if it had nothing to teach us concerning the nature of Heaven and hell. Consider the story's major components:

- When Lazarus died, angels carried him to Paradise.
- The rich man died and went to a place of torment. When Lazarus died, he went to a place of comfort.
- The present Heaven and hell are separated by a fixed chasm. In this case, people on both sides could see and communicate with each other, at least on a limited basis. (We shouldn't build a doctrine on this because it's not supported by other references.)
- The rich man, Abraham, and Lazarus all maintained their distinct identities from earth, indicating direct continuity from their earthly lives to their afterlives.
- The rich man and Lazarus had physical forms. The rich man had a tongue and a thirst that he wished to satisfy with water. Lazarus had a finger, and water was available to dip his finger.
- The rich man certainly remembers—and possibly sees—his lost brothers. He expresses concern for their welfare and asks that Lazarus be sent to warn them. This indicates consciousness after death and clear memory of earth and people on earth.

- Abraham says no one can cross the gap between Heaven and hell.
- Abraham explains that God's Word has been given to the brothers, and if they don't believe it, they wouldn't believe even if someone were sent back from the dead to warn them.

A strictly literal interpretation of this passage presses too far, suggesting things not taught elsewhere, such as that people in Heaven and hell talk to each other. Perhaps we should consider that every detail may not be literal but that Jesus intended for us to picture people in the afterlife as real humans with thoughts and capacities (and perhaps even forms) and with the same identity, memories, and awareness from their lives and relationships on earth. Surely Jesus intended us to envision both Heaven and hell as real places with real people from earth.

In the present Heaven or hell, we will await the time Jesus foretold, "when all who are in their graves will hear his voice and come out—those who have done good will rise to live, and those who have done evil will rise to be condemned" (John 5:28-29). Until that day comes, Scripture teaches that those who die will go to a real place, either the present Heaven or the present hell, as conscious human beings with memory of their lives and relationships on earth. Those in hell will live in misery, hopelessness, and apparent isolation while those in Heaven will live in comfort, joy, and rich relationship with God and others.

What has God shown you today that challenges your thinking or gives you encouragement to anticipate Heaven? _____

_____

_____

What concrete actions do you need to take in response to these insights? _____

_____

_____

_____

_____

_____

DAY 5

What Is Life Like in the Present Heaven?

We can make many observations about the present Heaven based on three key verses in Revelation 6. I trimmed my list to the following:

Read Revelation 6:9-11. Beside each of these brief observations, write *(A)* agree, *(D)* disagree, or *(U)* undecided.

___ 1. These people in Heaven were the same ones killed for Christ while on earth (v. 9). This demonstrates direct continuity between our identity on earth and our identity in Heaven.

___ 2. "They called out" (v. 10) means they could express themselves audibly. This suggests they exist in physical form, with vocal cords or other means to express themselves.

___ 3. They raised their voices (v. 10). This indicates that they are rational, communicative, and emotional—even passionate—beings, like people on earth.

___ 4. They called out in "a loud voice," not "loud voices." Individuals speaking with one voice indicate that Heaven is a place of unity and shared perspective.

___ 5. They ask God to intervene on earth and to act on their behalf (v. 10). "How long ... until you judge the inhabitants of the earth and avenge our blood?"

___ 6. They ask God questions, indicating they have much to learn. In Heaven, people desire and pursue understanding.

___ 7. They have a deep concern for justice and retribution (v. 10). In Heaven our concerns will be more passionate and our thirst for justice greater.

___ 8. Martyrs in Heaven pray for judgment on their persecutors who are still hurting others. They act in solidarity with and intercede for the suffering saints on earth, suggesting they both see and pray for saints on earth.

___ 9. Those in Heaven see God's attributes ("Sovereign ... holy and true") and understand His judgment of sin.

___ 10. Individuals are in Heaven: Each receives a white robe (v. 11). No merged identity obliterates uniqueness.

___ 11. Wearing white robes suggests possible physical forms because disembodied spirits don't wear robes.

___ 12. They have to "wait a little longer" (v. 11) in anticipation of the fulfillment of God's promises. Unlike the eternal Heaven—where no more sin, curse, or suffering exists (Rev. 21:4)—the present Heaven coexists with and watches over an earth under sin, the curse, and suffering.

___ 13. Time exists in the present Heaven (vv. 10-11). The martyrs ask: "How long, Sovereign Lord?" (v. 10).

___ 14. God knows all that is happening on earth (v. 11) including every suffering undergone by his children. He knows exactly how many martyrs will live, and he is prepared to return and set up his kingdom when the final martyr dies.

I've made these observations based on only three verses. I see no reason to believe that the realities of this passage apply only to one group of martyrs. We should assume that what is true of them is also true of our loved ones already there and will be true of us when we die.

Of those observations, which do you find:

1. most difficult to believe _____

_____

2. most encouraging _____

_____

The martyrs in Revelation 6 clearly remember at least some of what happened on earth. If they remember their martyrdom, there's no reason to assume they would forget other aspects of their earthly lives. In fact, we'll all likely remember much more in Heaven than we do on earth, and we will probably be able to see how God and His angels intervened on our behalf when we didn't realize it.

In Heaven, those who endured bad things on earth are comforted (see Luke 16:25). This implies memory of what happened. If we retain no memory of the bad things, why would we need such comfort?

About what painful event in your life would you want to have more clarity and perspective? _____

_____

About what positive area of your life do you look forward to learning more? _____

_____

Christ said, "There will be more rejoicing in heaven over one sinner who repents than over ninety-nine righteous persons who do not need to repent" (Luke 15:7). This rejoicing would logically include not only God but also the saints in Heaven who would so deeply appreciate the wonder of human conversion—especially the conversion of those they knew and loved on earth.

Many books on Heaven maintain that those in Heaven cannot be aware of people and events on earth because all the suffering and evil would make them unhappy; thus, Heaven would not truly be Heaven. I believe this argument is invalid. God knows exactly what's happening on earth, yet it doesn't diminish Heaven for Him. Likewise, it's Heaven for the angels, even though they also know what's happening on earth. In fact, angels in Heaven see the torment of hell, but it doesn't negate their joy in God's presence (see Rev. 14:10). Surely then, nothing they could see on earth could ruin Heaven for them.

It's also possible that even though joy predominates in the present Heaven, we could feel periodic sadness there because so much evil and pain still exists on earth. Christ grieved for people when He was on earth (see Matt. 23:37-39; John 11:33-36). Are we to think He no longer grieves because He's in Heaven? Or does He still hurt when His people suffer?

"Falling to the ground, he heard a voice saying to him, 'Saul, Saul, why are you persecuting Me?' 'Who are You, Lord?' he said. 'I am Jesus, whom you are persecuting' He replied." ACTS 9:4-5

In the margin circle the clear answer Acts 9:4-5 provides to that last question.

If Jesus in Heaven feels sorrow for His followers, might others there grieve as well? Going into the presence of Christ surely does not make us less compassionate. Revelation 21:4 refers specifically to the eternal Heaven. Christ's promise of no more tears or pain comes after "the old order of things has passed away" and there's no more suffering on earth.

What would you say to convince a friend that the occupants of Heaven are aware of events on earth?

_____

""He will wipe every tear from their eyes. There will be no more death or mourning or crying or pain, for the old order of things has passed away." REVELATION 21:4

The present and eternal Heavens are not the same. Though the present Heaven is far happier than earth under the curse, Scripture doesn't promise no sorrow there. People in Heaven are not frail beings whose joy can only be preserved by shielding them from truth. Happiness in Heaven is not based on ignorance but on perspective.

People in Christ's presence find joy in worshiping God and living in a sinless environment. Watching from Heaven, they have a great deal to praise God for, but they look forward to Christ's return, their resurrection, the final judgment, and the New Earth. Only then will we experience the fullness of joy purchased for us by Christ.

How would you explain the statement that happiness in Heaven is based not on ignorance but on perspective?

Happiness in Heaven is not based on ignorance but on perspective.

_____

Meanwhile, we can rejoice for our loved ones in Christ's presence. Our parting is not the end of our relationship, only an interruption. They are experiencing the joy of Christ's presence in a place so wonderful that Christ called it Paradise. And one day, we're told, in a magnificent reunion, they and we "will be with the Lord forever" (1 Thess. 4:17-18).

Grasping Redemption's Far Reach

DAY 1

Why Is Earth's Redemption Essential to God's Plan?

God created the entire universe to be an expression of His character. Because He is good, every facet of it was wonderful. But humanity rebelled, and the universe fell under the weight of our sin. Yet God did not give up on us. The serpent's seduction of Adam and Eve did not catch God by surprise. He had in place a plan by which He would redeem mankind—and all of creation—from sin, corruption, and death.

Just as He promises to make men and women new, He promises to renew the earth itself: "Behold, I will create new heavens and a new earth" (Isa. 65:17).

"In keeping with his promise we are looking forward to a new heaven and a new earth, the home of righteousness" (2 Pet. 3:13).

Many other passages allude to the New Heaven and New Earth without using those terms. God's redemptive plan climaxes not at the return of Christ nor in the millennial kingdom, but on the New Earth. Only then will all wrongs be made right. Only then will there be no more death, crying, or pain (Rev. 21:1-4).

God's kingdom and dominion are not about what happens in some remote, unearthly place; instead, they are about what happens on the earth God created for His glory. God has tied His glory to the earth and everything connected with it: mankind, animals, trees, rivers—everything. The earth is not disposable. It is essential to God's plan. God promises that ultimately the whole earth will be "filled with his glory" (Ps. 72:19; see Hab. 2:14).

What do you think it means that the earth will be filled with God's glory? _____

_____

_____

GOD'S EARTHLY RENEWAL PLAN

When Adam and Eve fell into sin, Satan appeared to have ruined God's plan for a righteous, undying humanity to rule the earth to God's glory. Yet immediately after the fall, God promised a human redeemer, the seed of the woman, who would one day come and crush the serpent (Gen. 3:15). While the wound of sin was still fresh, before the first scar had formed, God unveiled His plan to send a fully human redeemer who would be far more powerful than Satan. In a courageous act of intervention to deliver mankind, this redeemer would deliver a mortal wound to the usurping Devil and in the process would be wounded Himself.

God did not sit idly by nor shrug His shoulders at sin, death, and curse. He did not relinquish His claim on mankind and the earth. No sooner did ruin descend on humanity and earth than God revealed His plan to defeat Satan and retake them for His glory.

"I will put enmity between you and the woman, and between your offspring and hers; he will crush your head, and you will strike his heel." GENESIS 3:15

God has never given up on His original creation. Yet somehow we've managed to overlook an entire biblical vocabulary that makes this point clear. *Reconcile. Redeem. Restore. Regenerate. Recover. Return. Renew. Resurrect.* Each of these biblical words begins with the *re-* prefix, suggesting a return to an original condition that was ruined or lost.

To see examples of this, match the words on the left with their definitions.

1. __ resurrection   a. the reestablishment of a prior friendship or unity

2. __ renewal   b. becoming physically alive again, after death

3. __ reconciliation   c. to make new again, restoring to an original state

4. __ redemption   d. to buy back what was owned

These words emphasize that God always sees us in light of His original intention, and He always seeks to restore us to that design. Likewise, He sees the earth in terms of what He intended it to be, and He seeks to restore it to its original design. The answers are 1. b, 2. c, 3. a, 4. d.

If God had wanted to consign us to hell and start over, He could have. But He didn't. Instead, He chose to redeem what He started with—the heavens, earth, and mankind—to bring them back to His original purpose. God is the ultimate salvage artist. He loves to restore things to their original condition—and make them even better.

What part of your life are you most excited about God salvaging and restoring?

❏ physical health   ❏ moral purity

❏ conscience   ❏ His purpose

❏ other:_____

The hymn " 'Man of Sorrows,' What a Name" reflects God's purpose in our salvation with the phrase: "ruined sinners to reclaim!"[1] *Reclaim* is another *re-* word. It recognizes that God had a prior claim on humanity that was temporarily lost but is fully restored and taken to a new level in Christ. "The earth is the LORD's, and everything in it, the world, and all who live in it" (Ps. 24:1). God has never surrendered His title deed to the earth. He owns it—and He will not relinquish it to his enemies.

How do you feel about the personalized statement, "He owns me—and He will not relinquish me to His enemies"?

_____

_____

_____

God determined from the beginning that He will redeem mankind and restore the earth. Why? So His original plan will be fulfilled.

Scripture shows us God's purpose with remarkable clarity; yet for many years as a Bible student and pastor, I believed God was going to destroy the earth, abandon His original design and plan, and start over by implementing a new plan in an unearthly Heaven. Only in the past 15 years have my eyes been opened to what Scripture has said all along.

What lies behind our notion that God is going to destroy the earth and be done with it? I believe it's a weak theology of God. Though we'd never say it this way, we see Him as a thwarted inventor whose creation failed. Having realized His mistake, He'll end up trashing most of what He made. His consolation for a failed earth is that He rescues a few of us from the fire. But this idea is emphatically refuted by Scripture. God has a masterful plan, and He will not surrender earth to the trash heap.

THE NEW EARTH IS THE OLD EARTH RESTORED

Will the earth we know come to an end? Yes. To a final end? No. Revelation 21:1 says the old earth will pass away. But when people pass away, they do not cease to exist. As we will be raised to new life, so the earth will be raised to be a New Earth.

Did Peter invent the notion of all things being restored? No—he not only learned it from the prophets, he heard it directly from Christ. When Peter, hoping for commendation or reward, pointed out to Jesus that the disciples had left everything to follow him, the Lord didn't rebuke him. Instead, Jesus said, "At the renewal of all things, when the Son of Man sits on his glorious throne, you who have followed me will also sit on twelve thrones, judging the twelve tribes of Israel" (Matt. 19:28).

Note Christ's word choice. He did not say "after the destruction of all things" or "after the abandonment of all things" but "at the renewal of all things." This draws a line in the sand between two fundamentally different theologies. We were designed to live on the earth to God's glory.

Explain why God's glory demands that He succeed in renewing the earth. _____

_____

_____

Christ's incarnation, death, and resurrection secured a renewed humanity upon a renewed earth. Jesus explicitly said "all things" would be renewed (Matt. 19:28). Apart from those aspects of our present earthly lives that are inherently sinful or are fulfilled by a greater reality (more on this later), "all things" appears to be comprehensive.

The predominant belief that the ultimate Heaven God prepares for us will be unearthly could not be more unbiblical. Earth was made for people to live on, and people were made to live on earth.

God has His hands on the earth. He will not let go—even when it requires that His hands be pierced by nails. Both His incarnation and those nails secured Him to earth and its eternal future. In a redemptive work far larger than most imagine, Christ bought and paid for our future and the earth's. He died not only to make the best of a bad situation but also so that mankind, earth, and the universe itself would be renewed to forever proclaim His glory.

How can you respond to the realization both of God's future plan and the price He paid to bring it about?

_____

_____

_____

> *"Jesus said to them, 'I tell you the truth, at the renewal of all things, when the Son of Man sits on his glorious throne, you who have followed me will also sit on twelve thrones, judging the twelve tribes of Israel.'"*
> MATTHEW 19:28, NIV

Write a prayer expressing your thoughts to God for His refusal to give up on us or on His plans.

_____

_____

_____

_____

_____

DAY 2

Why Is the Resurrection So Important?

Jesus Christ's physical resurrection is the cornerstone of redemption—both for mankind and for the earth. Indeed, without Christ's resurrection and what it means—an eternal future for fully restored human beings dwelling on a fully restored earth—there would be no Christianity.

RESURRECTION IS PHYSICAL

I have found in many conversations that Christians tend to spiritualize the resurrection of the dead, effectively denying it. They don't reject it as a doctrine, but they deny its essential meaning: a permanent return to a physical existence in a physical universe.

Of Americans who believe in a resurrection of the dead, two-thirds believe they will not have bodies after the resurrection.[3] But this is self-contradictory. A nonphysical resurrection is like a sunless sunrise. There's no such thing. Resurrection means that we will have bodies. If we didn't have bodies, we wouldn't be resurrected!

Why does the bodily resurrection demand physical life on the New Earth? _____

_____

_____

The biblical doctrine of the resurrection of the dead begins with the human body but extends far beyond it. Theologian R. A. Torrey writes, "We will not be disembodied spirits in the world to come, but redeemed spirits, in redeemed bodies, in a redeemed universe."[4] If we don't get it right on the resurrection of the body, we'll get nothing else right. We must, therefore, understand and affirm the meaning of the resurrection.

Genesis 2:7 says, "The Lord God formed the man from the dust of the ground and breathed into his nostrils the breath of life, and the man became a living being." The Hebrew word for "living being" is *nephesh,* often translated "soul." The point at which Adam became *nephesh* is when God joined his body (dust) and spirit (breath) together. Adam was not a living human being until he had both physical and spiritual components. Thus the essence of humanity is spirit joined with body. Your body does not merely house the real you—it is as much a part of who you are as your spirit is.

God designed our bodies to be an integral part of our total being. Our physical bodies are an essential aspect of who we are, not just shells for our spirits to inhabit. Death is an abnormal condition because it tears apart what God created and joined together.

Those who believe in Platonism or in preexistent spirits see a disembodied soul as natural and even desirable. The Bible sees it as unnatural and undesirable. We are unified beings, and that is what we will be in eternity. That's why the bodily resurrection of the dead is so vital. And that's why Job rejoiced that in his flesh he would see God (Job 19:26).

When God sent Jesus to die, it was for our bodies as well as our spirits. He came to redeem not just "the breath of life" (spirit) but also "the dust of the ground" (body). When we die, it isn't that our real self goes to the intermediate Heaven and our fake self goes to the grave; it's that part of us goes to the intermediate Heaven and part goes to the grave to await our bodily resurrection.

We will never be all that God intended for us to be until body and spirit are again joined in resurrection. Any view of the afterlife that settles for less than a bodily resurrection—including christoplatonism, reincarnation, and transmigration of the soul—are explicitly unchristian.

"Even after my skin has been destroyed, yet I will see God in my flesh."

JOB 19:26, HCSB

Part of the reason for our incorrect thinking about bodily resurrection is that we fail to understand the environment in which resurrected people will live—the New Earth. Theologian Anthony Hoekema is right: "Resurrected bodies are not intended just to float in space, or to flit from cloud to cloud. They call for a *new earth* on which to live and to work, glorifying God. The doctrine of the resurrection of the body, in fact, makes no sense whatever apart from the doctrine of the new earth."[4]

CONTINUITY IS CRITICAL

Paul said if Christ didn't rise from the dead, we're still in our sins (see 1 Cor. 15:17)—meaning we'd be bound for hell, not Heaven. He didn't just say that the Christian life is futile without Heaven. He said if there's no resurrection of the dead, then the hope of Christianity is an illusion, and we're to be pitied for placing our faith in Christ. Paul had no interest in a Heaven that's merely for human spirits. Ultimately, there is no Heaven for human spirits unless Heaven is also for human bodies.

When I came to Christ as a high school student, I became a new person (2 Cor. 5:17), yet I was still the same person. My mother saw a lot of changes, but she still said, "Good morning, Randy," not "Who are you?" I was still me, though a substantially transformed version.

Conversion does not mean eliminating the old but transforming it. Despite the radical changes that occur through salvation, death, and resurrection, we remain who we are. We have the same history, appearance, memory, interests, and skills. This is the principle of redemptive continuity. God is not going to scrap His original creation and start over. He will take His fallen children and restore us to our original design.

What most excites you about being restored to God's original design? _____

_____

_____

The New Earth will still be earth, but a changed earth. Just as those reborn through salvation maintain continuity with the people they were, so too the world will be reborn in continuity with the old world.

If we don't grasp the principle of redemptive continuity, we cannot understand the nature of our resurrection.

THE NATURE OF OUR NEW BODIES

When Jesus said to His disciples after His resurrection, "It is I myself," He was emphasizing to them that He was the same person—in spirit and body—who had gone to the cross (Luke 24:39). His disciples saw the marks of His crucifixion, unmistakable evidence that this was the same body.

Our resurrected bodies are the same bodies but raised to greater perfection than we've ever known. Because we each have a physical body, we already have the single best reference point for envisioning a new body. It's like the new upgrade I bought of my word processing software. When I heard an upgrade was available, I didn't say, "I have no idea what it will be like." I knew that for the most part it would be like the old program. Sure, it has some new features that I didn't expect, and I'm glad for them. But I certainly recognize it as the same program I've used for a decade.

Likewise, when we receive our resurrected bodies, we'll no doubt have some welcome surprises. Maybe we'll even have some new features (though no glitches or programming errors!), but we'll certainly recognize our new bodies as being ours. God has given us working models to guide our imagination about what our new bodies will be like on the New Earth.

CHRIST'S RESURRECTED LIFE
IS THE MODEL FOR OURS

Not only do we know what our present bodies are like, but we also have an example in Scripture of what a resurrection body is like. We're told a great deal about Christ's resurrected body, and we're told that our bodies will be like His.

"Dear friends, now we are children of God, and what we will be has not yet been made known. But we know that when he appears, we shall be like him, for we shall see him as he is" (1 John 3:2).

"The Lord Jesus Christ ... will transform our lowly bodies so that they will be like his glorious body" (Phil. 3:20–21).

"And just as we have borne the likeness of the earthly man, so shall we bear the likeness of the man from heaven" (1 Cor. 15:49).

Which was the difference between Adam and Christ?

❏ One was a physical being and the other wasn't.

❏ Adam was under sin and the curse and Christ was not.

Jesus was and is a human being, "in every respect like us" (Heb. 2:17, NLT), except with respect to sin. Though Jesus in His resurrected body proclaimed, "I am not a ghost" (Luke 24:39, NLT), countless Christians think they will be ghosts in the eternal Heaven. They think they'll be disembodied spirits or wraiths. The magnificent, cosmos-shaking victory of Christ's resurrection—by definition a physical triumph over physical death in a physical world—escapes them. If Jesus had been a ghost, if we would be ghosts; redemption wouldn't have been accomplished.

What do you remember from Scripture about what Jesus did in His resurrection body? (If you need a hint, see John 21.)

_____

_____

By observing the resurrected Christ, we learn not only about resurrected bodies but also about resurrected relationships. Christ communicated with His disciples and showed His love to them as a group and as individuals. He instructed them and entrusted a task to them.

If you study Jesus' interactions with Mary Magdalene (John 20:10-18), Thomas (vv. 24-29), and Peter (21:15-22), you will see how similar they are to His interactions with these same people before He died. The fact that Jesus picked up His relationships where they'd left off is a foretaste of our own lives after we are resurrected. In both the present Heaven and the New Earth, we will experience continuity between our current lives and our resurrected lives, with the same memories and relational histories.

Inside your body, even if it is failing, is the blueprint for your resurrection body. You may not be satisfied with your current body or mind—but you'll be thrilled with your resurrection upgrades. With them you'll be better able to serve and glorify God and to enjoy an eternity of wonders He has prepared for you.

D A Y   3

What Will It Mean for the Curse to be Lifted?

Without understanding God's original plan, we cannot fully understand His future plan. Consider the three phases of earth's history:

1. Creation was perfect, though with the potential for evil.
2. Mankind's fall and first judgment (Gen. 3), the earth's first radical transition, forms the backbone of human history as we know it.
3. In the earth's last radical transition (Rev. 20) Christ's return and last judgment brings the conclusion to humanity's story.

Other parallels in Scripture help us grasp our current condition.

- In Genesis, God planted the garden on earth; in Revelation, He brings down the New Jerusalem, with a garden at its center, to the New Earth.
- In Eden, there's no sin, death, or curse; on the New Earth, there's no more sin, death, or curse.
- In Genesis, the Redeemer is promised; in Revelation, the Redeemer returns. Genesis tells the story of Paradise lost; Revelation tells the story of Paradise regained.
- In Genesis, humanity's stewardship is squandered; in Revelation, humanity's stewardship is triumphant, empowered by the human and divine King Jesus.

These parallels are too remarkable to be anything but deliberate. These mirror images demonstrate the perfect symmetry of God's plan. We live in the in-between time, hearing echoes of Eden and the approaching footfalls of the New Earth.

REMOVING THE CURSE

The earth as it is now is not our home. The world as it was, and as it will be, is. We have never known a world without sin, suffering, and death. Yet we yearn for such a life and such a world. When we see a roaring waterfall, beautiful flowers, animals in their native habitat, or the joy in the eyes of our pets when they see us, we sense that this world is—or at least was meant to be—our home.

If the Bible said nothing else about life in the eternal Heaven, the New Earth, these words would tell us a vast amount: "No longer will there be any curse" (Rev. 22:3). What would our lives be like if the curse were lifted? One day we will know firsthand.

How does the curse affect your life in some of the following areas?

1. life Purpose
4. health
2. relationships
5. inner life (your thoughts and feelings)
3. work

_____

_____

_____

_____

How do you see the removal of the curse changing your life?

_____

_____

After Adam sinned, God said, "Cursed is the ground [earth] because of you" (Gen. 3:17). When the curse is reversed, we will no longer engage in "painful toil" (v. 17) but will enjoy satisfying caretaking. No longer will the earth yield "thorns and thistles" (v. 18), defying our dominion and repaying us for corrupting it. No longer will we "return to the ground ... [from which we] were taken" (v. 19), swallowed up in death as unrighteous stewards who ruined ourselves and the earth. Death, though a curse in itself, was also the only way out from under the curse—and that only because God had a way to defeat death and to restore mankind's relationship with Him.

THE LAST ADAM DEFEATS SATAN

Christ is the last Adam, who will undo the damage wrought by the first Adam. He came to remove the curse of sin and death (Rom. 8:2). Romans 5:12-19 lays out the consequences of Adam's sin and the redeeming work of Jesus Christ, the last Adam.

Satan successfully tempted the first Adam. When Satan tempted the last Adam in the wilderness, which is what Eden's garden had become, Christ resisted him.

The Evil One was desperate to defeat Christ, to kill Him as he had the first Adam (Matt. 4:1-11; Luke 4:1-13). Satan appeared to succeed when the last Adam died, but Jesus didn't die because He had sinned. He died because He chose to pay the price for our sins. Satan's apparent victory in Christ's death actually assured the Devil's final defeat. When Christ rose from the dead, He dealt Satan a fatal blow, assuring both his destruction and the resurrection of mankind and the earth. Satan's grip on this world was loosened. It's still strong, but once he is cast into the lake of fire earth will slip forever from Satan's grasping hands, never again to be touched by him (Rev. 20:10).

Christ has already defeated Satan, but the full scope of his victory has not yet been manifested on earth. At Christ's ascension, God "seated him at his right hand in the heavenly realms ... And God placed all things under his feet and appointed him to be head over everything" (Eph. 1:20-22). These words are all-inclusive, and they are past tense, not future. Christ rules the universe. And yet Satan will be bound only upon Christ's physical return to the earth.

Check the statements that are true about the Last Adam.

❑ Jesus passed the test that Adam failed.
❑ Christ's death seemed to be defeat but was a great victory.
❑ The last Adam died to pay for our sin.
❑ The full scope of Christ's victory appeared in His resurrection.

Life on the present earth is an "already and not yet" paradox. Heaven's king is even now "ruler of the kings of the earth" (Rev. 1:5). In the cross

> Jesus didn't die because He had sinned. He died because He chose to pay the price for our sins.

and the resurrection, God made a way not only to restore His original design but also to expand it. All but the last statement are true.

In bringing us salvation, Christ has already undone some of the damage in our hearts; in the end He will finally and completely restore His entire creation to what God originally intended (Rom. 8:19-21). Christ will turn back the curse and restore to humanity all that we lost in Eden, and He will give us much more besides.

UNITING HEAVEN AND EARTH

God's plan of the ages is "to bring all things in heaven and on earth together under one head, even Christ" (Eph. 1:10). "All things" is broad and inclusive—nothing will be left out. This verse corresponds precisely to the culmination of history in Revelation 21, the merging of the once separate realms of Heaven and earth, fully under Christ's lordship.

As God and man will be forever united in Jesus, so Heaven and earth will forever be united in the new physical universe where we will live as resurrected beings. To affirm anything less is to understate the redemptive work of Christ. Yet, strangely, in the schools and churches I've been a part of—and in the vast majority of the 150 books about Heaven I've read—this central truth has rarely been affirmed.

Heaven is God's home. Earth is our home. Jesus Christ, as the God-man, forever links God and mankind, and thereby forever links Heaven and earth. Christ will make earth into Heaven and Heaven into earth. Just as the wall that separates God and humanity is torn down in Jesus, so too the wall that separates Heaven and earth will be forever demolished. In one universe all things in Heaven and on earth will be brought together under one head, Jesus Christ (Rev. 21:3).

God's plan is that no more gulf will separate the spiritual and physical worlds. One universe will be united under one Lord—forever. This is the unstoppable plan of God. This is where history is headed.

When God walked with Adam and Eve in the garden, earth was Heaven's backyard. The New Earth will be even more than that—it will be Heaven itself. And those who know Jesus will live there.

"Now the dwelling of God is with men, and he will live with them."
REVELATION 21:3

What has God shown you today that makes you anticipate Heaven and willing to serve Christ sacrificially now?

_____

_____

_____

DAY 4

What Does the Restored Earth Mean?

If God were to end history and reign forever in a distant Heaven, earth would be remembered as a graveyard of sin and failure. Instead, earth will be redeemed, and become a far greater world, even for having gone through the birth pains of suffering and sin. The New Earth will justify the old earth's disaster, make good out of it, and put it in perspective.

BUT DOESN'T SCRIPTURE SAY THAT THE EARTH WILL BE DESTROYED?

At first glance, some Scriptures seem to suggest the present earth and the entire universe will be utterly destroyed: Psalm 102:25-26 says the heavens and earth will "perish" and be "discarded." Second Peter 3:10 says they will be "destroyed by fire" and "laid bare." Revelation 21:1 declares they had "passed away."

In contrast, some passages speak of the earth remaining forever (see Eccl. 1:4; Ps. 78:69). The same earth destined for destruction is also destined for restoration. Many have grasped the first teaching but not the second. Therefore, they misapply the word *destroy* to mean absolute or final destruction, rather than what Scripture actually teaches: a temporary destruction, reversed through resurrection and restoration.

John Piper argued, "When Revelation 21:1 and 2 Peter 3:10 say that the present earth and heavens will 'pass away,' it does not have to mean that they go out of existence, but may mean that there will be such a

> *"He built His sanctuary like the heights, like the earth that He established forever."*
>
> PSALM 78:69, HCSB

change in them that their present condition passes away. We might say, 'The caterpillar passes away, and the butterfly emerges.' There is a real passing away, and there is a real continuity, a real connection."[2]

My wife, Nanci, and I will never forget driving home from church on May 18, 1980, and seeing a cloud of volcanic ash from the eruption of Mount Saint Helens, 70 miles from our home. The destruction of the beautiful mountain and its surrounding area was catastrophic. Great trees were charred and fallen like giant matchsticks. Experts predicted it would certainly be decades, possibly centuries, before the area came back to life. Yet within only a few years it had begun to be restored, demonstrating the healing properties God has built into his creation, evident even under the curse.

After seeing such utter devastation replaced by new beauty—even apart from God's supernatural intervention—I have no trouble envisioning God remaking a charred earth into a new one, fresh and vibrant. The earth will be raised to new life in the same way our bodies will be raised to new life.

After all, what thrilled early, expectant believers was not that God would rule in Heaven—He already did. Their hope was that one day He would rule on earth. They believed the Messiah would make God's will be done on earth as it is in Heaven. Like the ancient Israelites, they longed for God's rule on earth, not just for a hundred years or a thousand but forever. The preoccupation with God's establishment of an earthly kingdom couldn't be more clear than in Isaiah 65.

In the following passage, underline phrases that indicate that the prophecy in Isaiah 65 refers to the New Earth.

> "'For I will create a new heaven and a new earth ...
> Then be glad and rejoice forever
> in what I am creating;
> for I will create Jerusalem to be a joy,
> and its people to be a delight.
> I will rejoice in Jerusalem
> and be glad in My people.

> The sound of weeping and crying
> will no longer be heard in her.
> People will build houses and live |in them|;
> they will plant vineyards and eat their fruit.
> The wolf and the lamb will feed together,
> and the lion will eat straw like the ox,
> but the serpent's food will be dust!
> They will not do what is evil or destroy
> on My entire holy mountain,'
> says the LORD." *Isaiah 65:17-19,21,25, HCSB*

The new, restored earth, will be the setting for God's kingdom. People will come to pay Him tribute in the New Jerusalem: "'As the new heavens and the new earth that I make will endure before me,' declares the LORD, 'so will your name and descendants endure. ... All mankind will come and bow down before me,' says the LORD" (Isa. 66:22-23).

God has a future plan for the earth and a future plan for Jerusalem. His plan involves an actual kingdom over which He and His people will reign—not merely for a thousand years but forever (see Rev. 22:5). It will be the long delayed but never derailed fulfillment of God's command for mankind to exercise righteous dominion over the earth.

THE MESSIAH'S EARTHLY KINGDOM

God's people were right to expect the Messiah to bring an earthly kingdom. That's exactly what God promised: "All kings shall fall down before Him; All nations shall serve Him" (Ps. 72:11, NKJV). An explicitly messianic passage tells us, "His rule will extend from sea to sea and from the River to the ends of the earth" (Zech. 9:10).

Isaiah 66 says that peace will come to Jerusalem and Jerusalem will become a center of all nations. "'I ... am about to come and gather all nations and tongues, and they will come and see my glory.' ... 'As the new heavens and the new earth that I make will endure before me,' declares the LORD, 'so will your name and descendants endure. ... All mankind will come and bow down before me,' says the LORD" (Isa. 66:18,22-23).

This prophecy, like the others, is clearly fulfilled in Revelation. Because this Jerusalem will reside on the New Earth, wouldn't we expect it to be called the New Jerusalem? That's exactly what it is called (see Rev. 3:12; 21:2). Scripture's repeated promises about land, peace, and the centrality of Jerusalem among all cities and nations will be fulfilled.

If a millennial reign on earth precedes the New Earth, it could offer a foretaste. However, regardless of the proper understanding of the Millennium, the ultimate fulfillment of a host of Old Testament prophecies will be on the New Earth, where the people of God will "possess the land *forever*" (Isa. 60:21, emphasis added).

Are you surprised to realize what detailed descriptions of Heaven the Scripture contains? ❑ yes ❑ no

In what way does this review of Scripture cause you to think differently about Heaven?

_____

_____

_____

_____

REDEMPTION MEANS RESTORATION

Even if the term *New Earth* appeared nowhere in Scripture, even if we didn't have dozens of other passages such as Isaiah 60 that refer to it so clearly, Acts 3:21 would be sufficient. It tells us that Christ will "remain in heaven until the time comes for God to restore everything, as he promised long ago through his holy prophets." When Christ returns, God's agenda is to "restore everything." The perfection of creation once lost will be fully regained, and then some. The same Peter who spoke these words in Acts 3 wrote the words about the earth's destruction in 2 Peter 3, and he apparently saw no conflict between them.

The key to understanding the images of destruction in 2 Peter lies within the passage itself. Peter drew a parallel between the earth in the time of Noah, which was "destroyed" through the flood, and the time to come when the present world will be destroyed in judgment again, this time not by water but by fire (2 Pet. 3:6-7). The stated reference point for understanding the future destruction of the world is the flood. It did not obliterate the world, making it cease to exist. Noah and his family and the animals were delivered from God's judgment to reinhabit a new world made ready for them by God's cleansing judgment.

The cleansing with fire will be more thorough than the flood in that it will permanently eliminate sin. But just as God's judgment by water didn't make the earth permanently uninhabitable, neither will God's judgment by fire.

THE MEANING OF "NEW"

As God may gather the scattered DNA and atoms and molecules of our bodies, He will regather all He needs of the scorched and disfigured earth. As our old bodies will be raised to new bodies, so the old earth will be raised to become the New Earth. So, will the earth be destroyed or renewed? The answer is both—but the "destruction" will be temporal and partial, whereas the renewal will be eternal and complete.

The doctrine of the new creation extends not only to people but to the world, the natural realm, and even nations and cultures. The new creation is a major biblical theme, though you might never know it judging by how little attention it receives among Christians.

How would you respond to the person who dismisses a future on the New Earth with the claim that the earth will be destroyed?

_____

_____

_____

The earth's death will be no more final than our own. The destruction of the old earth in God's purifying judgment will immediately be followed by its resurrection to new life. Earth's fiery "end" will open straight into a glorious new beginning. And as we'll see later, it will just keep getting better and better.

DAY 5

Will the New Earth Feel Like Home?

Sometimes when we look at this world's breathtaking beauty we feel a twinge of disappointment. Why? Because we know we're going to leave this behind. In consolation or self-rebuke, we might say, "This world is not my home." But if we were honest we might add, "But part of me sure wishes it were."

What we really want is to live forever in a world with all the beauty and none of the ugliness—a world without sin, death, the curse, and all the personal and relational problems and disappointments they create.

We who emphasize our citizenship in Heaven sometimes minimize our connection to the earth and our destiny to live on and rule it. We end up thinking of eternity as a nonearthly spiritual state.

What we have assumed about Heaven has reduced it to a place we look forward to only as an alternative to an intolerable existence here. Only the elderly, disabled, suffering, and persecuted might desire the Heaven we imagine. But the Bible portrays life in our resurrected bodies in a resurrected universe, as so exciting and compelling that even the youngest and healthiest of us should daydream about it.

Really use your imagination. What do you look forward to doing on the New Earth that you've never gotten to do here?

_____

_____

_____

We long for home, even as we step out to explore undiscovered new frontiers. We long for the familiarity of the old, even as we crave the innovation of the new. Think of all the things we love that are new: moving into a new house, the smell of a new car, the feel of a new book, a new movie, a new song, the pleasure of a new friend, the enjoyment of a new pet, arriving at a new school or a new workplace, welcoming a new child or grandchild, eating new foods that suit our tastes.

We love newness—yet in each case what is new is attached to something familiar. We don't really like things utterly foreign to us. Instead, we appreciate fresh and innovative variations on things that we already know and love. So when we hear that in Heaven we will have new bodies and live on a New Earth, that's how we should understand the word *new*—a restored and perfected version of the familiar.

Understanding and anticipating the physical nature of the New Earth corrects a multitude of errors. It frees us to love the world that God has made, without guilt, while saying no to the world corrupted by our sin. It reminds us that God Himself gave us the earth, gave us a love for the earth, and will give us the New Earth.

HOMESICK AT HOME

Do you recall a time when you were away from your earthly home and desperately missed it? Do you remember how your heart ached for home? That's how we should feel about Heaven. We are a displaced people, longing for our home. C. S. Lewis said, "If I find in myself a desire which no experience in this world can satisfy, the most probable explanation is that I was made for another world."[4]

Nothing is more often misdiagnosed than our homesickness for Heaven. We think that what we want is sex, drugs, alcohol, a new job, a raise, a spouse, a new car, or a cabin in the woods. What we really want is the person we were made for—Jesus—and the place we were made for—Heaven. Nothing less can satisfy us.

A Christian I met in passing once told me it troubled him that he really didn't long for Heaven. He didn't desire a Heaven out there somewhere but an earth under his feet where God was glorified. He felt guilty and unspiritual for this desire.

At the time, my eyes hadn't been opened to Scripture's promise of the New Earth. If I could talk with that man again, I'd tell him what I should have told him the first time—that his longing was biblical and right. In fact, the place he's always longed for, an earth where God was fully glorified, is where he will live forever.

To say "This world is not your home" to a person who is fully alive and alert to the wonders of the world is like throwing a bucket of water on kindling's blaze. Instead, we should fan the flames of that blaze to help it spread, not seek to put it out. Otherwise we malign our God-given instinct to love the earthly home God made for us. And we reduce "spirituality" into a denial of art, culture, science, sports, education, and all else human.

When we do this, we set ourselves up for hypocrisy. We turn on our favorite music, watch a ball game, play golf, ride bikes, work in the garden, or curl up with a good book—not because we are sinners but because we are people. We will still be people when we die and go to Heaven. This isn't a disappointing reality—it's God's plan. He made us as we are—except the sin part, which has nothing to do with friends, eating, sports, gardening, or reading.

We get tired of ourselves, of others, of sin and suffering and crime and death. Yet we love the earth, don't we? I love the spaciousness of the night sky over the ocean. I love the coziness of sitting next to Nanci on the couch in front of the fireplace. These experiences are not Heaven—but they are foretastes of Heaven. What we love about this life are the things that resonate with the life we were made for. The things we love are not merely the best this life has to offer—they are previews of the greater life to come.

What do we gain when we celebrate the foretastes of Heaven God has given us?

_____

_____

_____

_____

1. Maltbie D. Babcock, "This Is My Father's World," _The Baptist Hymnal_ (Nashville: Convention Press, 1991), 43.
2. John Piper, _Future Grace_ (Sisters, OR: Multnomah, 1995), 371, 376.
3. Ibid., 376.
4. C. S. Lewis, _Mere Christianity_ (New York: Collier, 1960), 120.

Celebrating the Joy and Industry of the New Earth

DAY 1

What Will It Mean to See God?

GOD'S GREATEST GIFT TO US

Our longing for Heaven is a longing for God. Being with God is the heart and soul of Heaven. Every other heavenly pleasure will derive from and be secondary to His presence. God's greatest gift to us is, and always will be, Himself.

God "lives in unapproachable light, whom no one has seen or can see" (1 Tim. 6:16). In Scripture, to see God's face was utterly unthinkable. That's why, when we're told we'll see God's face (see Rev. 22:4), it should astound us. For this to happen would require radical change in us. To be welcomed into the presence of our Lord shall be the wonder of our redemption. The blood of Jesus has bought us full access to God's throne room and His most holy place. Even now,

He welcomes us to come there in prayer. In eternity we will live in his presence as resurrected beings.

WILL WE SEE THE FACES OF BOTH THE FATHER AND THE SON?

God, who is transcendent, became immanent in Jesus Christ. So whenever we see Jesus in Heaven, we will see God. Because Jesus Christ is a permanent manifestation of God, he could say to Philip, "Anyone who has seen me has seen the Father" (John 14:9). Certainly, then, a primary way we will see the Father on the New Earth is through His Son, Jesus.

Yet Jesus said, "Blessed are the pure in heart, for they will see God" (Matt. 5:8). And in Revelation 22:4, when it says "they will see his face," it appears to refer to seeing the face of God the Father.

Imagine the moment when you see Jesus face-to-face. How do you expect to react? _____

_____

_____

Would your reaction to seeing God the Father's face be any different than seeing Jesus? ❑ yes ❑ no ❑ I'm not sure. **Why?**

_____

_____

_____

SEEING GOD: OUR PRIMARY JOY

In Heaven the barriers between redeemed human beings and God will forever be gone. To look into God's eyes will be to see what we've always longed to see: the One who made us for His own good pleasure. Seeing God will be like seeing everything else for the first time because we'll not only see God but He also will be the lens through which we see everything else—people, ourselves, and the events of this life.

The essence of eternal life is "that they may know you, the only true God, and Jesus Christ, whom you have sent" (John 17:3). Our primary joy in Heaven will be knowing and seeing God. Every other joy will be derivative, flowing from the fountain of our relationship with God.

Asaph's statement in Psalm 73:25 may seem an overstatement—there's nothing on earth this man desires but God? But he's affirming that the central desires of our heart are for God. Yes, we desire many other things—but in desiring them, it is really God we desire. Augustine called God "the end of our desires." He prayed, "You have made us for yourself, O Lord, and our hearts are restless until they rest in you."[1]

Suppose you're sick. Your friend brings a meal. What meets your needs—the meal or the friend? Both. Of course, without your friend, there would be no meal; but even without a meal, you would still treasure your friendship. Hence, your friend is both your higher pleasure and the source of your secondary pleasure (the meal). Likewise, God is the source of all lesser goods so that when they satisfy us, it's God Himself who satisfies us.

When I speak elsewhere in the study of the joys of the resurrected life, some readers may think, *But our eyes should be on the giver, not the gift; we must focus on God, not on Heaven.* This approach sounds spiritual, but it erroneously divorces our experience of God from life, relationships, and the world—all of which God graciously gives us. It sees the material realm and other people as God's competitors rather than as instruments that communicate His love and character.

When you give a gift, does the recipient's joy:

❑ make you jealous   ❑ upset you   ❑ bring you joy

Though some frown on the pleasures of the physical world, mistaking asceticism for spirituality, Scripture says we are to put our hope not in material things but "in God, who richly provides us with everything for our enjoyment" (1 Tim. 6:17). If He provides everything for our enjoyment, we shouldn't feel guilty for enjoying it, should we?

Paul said demons and liars portray the physical realm as unspiritual, forbid people from the joys of marriage, including sex, and "order them to abstain from certain foods, which God created to be received with thanksgiving by those who believe and who know the truth. For

"Whom have I in heaven but you? And earth has nothing I desire besides you." PSALM 73:25

asceticism

the religious doctrine that one can reach a higher spiritual state by rigorous self-discipline and self-denial everything God created is good, and nothing is to be rejected if it is received with thanksgiving, because it is consecrated by the word of God and prayer" (1 Tim. 4:3-5).

Because of the current darkness of our hearts, we must be careful not to make idols out of God's provisions. But once we're freed from sin and in God's presence, we'll never have to worry about putting people or things above God. That would be unthinkable. It would be unthinkable to us now if we were thinking clearly.

God isn't displeased when we enjoy a good meal, marital sex, a football game, a cozy fire, or a good book. He's not up in Heaven frowning at us and saying, "Stop it—you should only find joy in Me." This would be as foreign to God's nature as our Heavenly Father as it would be to mine as an earthly father if I gave my daughters a Christmas gift and started pouting because they enjoyed it too much. No, I gave the gift to bring joy to them and to me. If they didn't take pleasure in it, I'd be disappointed. Their pleasure in my gift to them draws them closer to me. I am delighted that they enjoyed the gift.

Of course, if children become so preoccupied with the gift that they walk away from their father and ignore him, that would be different. Though preoccupation with a God-given gift can turn into idolatry, enjoying that same gift with a grateful heart can draw us closer to God. In Heaven we'll have no capacity to turn people or things into idols. When we find joy in God's gifts, we will be finding our joy in Him.

All secondary joys are derivative in nature. They cannot be separated from God. Flowers are beautiful because God is beautiful. Rainbows are stunning because God is stunning. Puppies are delightful because God is delightful. Sports are fun because God is fun. Study is rewarding because God is rewarding. Work is fulfilling because God is fulfilling.

For those who struggle under a persistent cloud of guilt, how might understanding God's joyful nature help them love Him and enjoy His gracious gifts? _____

_____

_____

_____

God is a lavish giver. The God who gave us His Son delights to graciously give us "all things." These "all things" are in addition to Christ, but they are never instead of Him—they come "along with Him." If we didn't have Christ, we would have nothing. But because we have Christ, we have everything. Hence we can enjoy the people and things God has made and in the process enjoy the God who designed and provided them for His pleasure and ours.

God welcomes prayers of thanksgiving for meals, warm fires, games, books, sex, and every other good thing. When we fail to acknowledge God as the source of all good things, we fail to give Him the recognition and glory He deserves. We separate God from joy, which is like trying to separate heat from fire or wetness from rain.

Every day we should see God in His creation—in the food we eat, the air we breathe, the friendships we enjoy, and the pleasures of family, work, and hobbies. Yes, we must sometimes forgo secondary pleasures, and we should never let them eclipse God. But we should thank Him for all of life's joys, large and small, and allow them to draw us to Him.

That's exactly what we'll do in Heaven, so why not start now?

Look out a window, flip through an old photo album, or spend the afternoon playing with your kids. As you do, note details and memories in the experience that bring you joy. Praise God for each thing that comes to mind.

> *"He who did not spare his own Son, but gave him up for us all—how will he not also, along with him, graciously give us all things?"*
> ROMANS 8:32

THE THRILL TO COME

Beholding and knowing God, we will spend eternity worshiping, exploring, and serving Him, seeing His magnificent beauty in everything and everyone around us. In the new universe, as we study nature, as we pursue science and mathematics and every realm of knowledge, we'll see God in everything, for He's behind it all.

Eden's greatest attraction was God's presence. The greatest tragedy of sin and the curse was that God no longer dwelt with His people. His presence came back in a small but real way in the Holy of Holies in the tabernacle and in the temple. After the exile, Ezekiel saw God's *shekinah* glory—His visible presence—leave the temple and the city, a sad day for Israel (see Ezek. 11:23).

God's *shekinah* glory returned in Christ, who tabernacled among us (took up temporary residence); "We have seen his glory" (John 1:14). God's glory resides now in His people, the temple He indwells (1 Cor. 3:17). But one day Christ will come and make a new people, a New Earth, and a new universe in which He will dwell among His people, fully and freely. All else—in this world and the next—will be secondary to beholding our Lord. To see Jesus—what could be greater? "We shall be like him, for we shall see him as he is" (1 John 3:2).

We will see Christ in His glory. The most exhilarating experiences on earth, such as white-water rafting, skydiving, or extreme sports, will seem tame compared to the thrill of seeing Jesus.

Being with Him. Gazing at Him. Talking with Him. Worshiping Him. Embracing Him. Eating with Him. Walking with Him. Laughing with Him. Imagine it.

DAY 2

What Will It Mean for God to Dwell Among Us?

THE JOY OF A GOD-CENTERED HEAVEN

Consider this statement: "God himself will be with them" (Rev. 21:3). Why does it emphatically say "God himself"? Because God won't merely send us a delegate. He will actually come to live among us on the New Earth. As writer Steven J. Lawson explained, "God's glory will fill and permeate the entire new Heaven, not just one centralized place. Thus, wherever we go in Heaven, we will be in the immediate presence of the full glory of God. Wherever we go, we will enjoy the complete manifestation of God's presence. Throughout all eternity, we will never be separated from direct, unhindered fellowship with God."[2]

God's glory will be the air we breathe, and we'll always try to breathe deeper to gain more of it. We'll never be able to travel far enough to leave God's presence. If we could, we'd never want to. However great the wonders of Heaven, God Himself is Heaven's greatest prize.

BEING WITH JESUS

Jesus promised His disciples, "I will come back and take you to be with me that you also may be where I am" (John 14:3). For Christians, to die is to "be present with the Lord" (2 Cor. 5:8, NKJV). The Apostle Paul said, "I desire to depart and be with Christ, which is better by far" (Phil. 1:23). He could have said, "I desire to depart and be in Heaven," but He didn't—His mind was on being with His Lord Jesus, which is the most significant aspect of Heaven.

Jesus called His disciples "friends" (John 15:15). He's also our best friend, and when we see Him face-to-face, we'll never doubt it. We'll worship Him as the Almighty and bow to Him in reverence, yet we'll never sense His disapproval—because we'll never disappoint Him. He'll never be unhappy with us. We'll be able to relax in Heaven. No skeletons will fall out of our closets. Christ bore every one of our sins. He paid the ultimate price so that we would be forever free from sin—and the fear of sin. All barriers between us and Him will be forever gone.

When Jesus prays that we will be with Him in Heaven, He explained why: "Father, I want those you have given me to be with me where I am, and to see my glory, the glory you have given me because you loved me before the creation of the world" (John 17:24). When we accomplish something, we want to share it with those closest to us. Likewise, Jesus wants to share with us His glory—His person and His accomplishments.

Name an accomplishment you have wanted to share.

_____

_____

With whom did you most want to share it?

_____

There's no contradiction between Christ acting for His glory and for our good. The two are synonymous. Our greatest pleasure, our greatest satisfaction, is to behold his glory. As John Piper said, "God is most glorified in us when we are most satisfied in him."[3]

Meditate for a moment on how you feel when you bring someone else joy. Describe your feelings.

_____

_____

How are your feelings related to your love for that person?

_____

_____

Christ's desire for us to see His glory should touch us deeply. What an unexpected compliment that the Creator of the universe has gone to such great lengths, at such sacrifice, to prepare a place for us where we can behold and participate in His glory.

Jesus indwells us now, and perhaps He will then, but He will also physically reside on the earth with us. Have you ever imagined what it would be like to walk the earth with Jesus as the disciples did? Have you ever wished you had that opportunity? You will—on the New Earth. Whatever we will do with Jesus, we'll be doing with the second member of the Trinity. What will it be like to run beside God, laugh with God, discuss a book with God, sing and climb and play catch with God?

Jesus promised we would eat with Him in His kingdom. This is an intimacy unthinkable to any who don't grasp the significance of the Incarnation. To eat a meal with Jesus will be to eat a meal with God.

WILL GOD SERVE US?

Jesus said, "It will be good for those servants whose master finds them watching when he comes. I tell you the truth, he will dress himself to serve, will have them recline at the table and will come and wait on them" (Luke 12:37).

Jesus said the Master will do something culturally unthinkable—become a servant to His servants because He loves them and also out of appreciation for their loyalty and service to Him. The King becomes a servant, making His servants kings! Notice that He won't merely command His other servants to serve them. He will do it Himself.

We will be in Heaven only because "the Son of Man did not come to be served, but to serve, and to give his life as a ransom for many" (Matt. 20:28). We must assent to Christ's service for us. But even in Heaven, it appears, Jesus will sometimes serve us. What greater and more amazing reward could be ours in the new universe than to have Jesus choose to serve us?

In what ways is Jesus already fulfilling this promise to serve us every day? Plan to discuss this in your group.

_____

_____

_____

_____

If it were our idea that God would serve us, it would be blasphemy. But it's His idea. As husbands serve their wives and parents serve their children, God desires to serve us. "On this mountain the LORD Almighty will prepare a feast of rich food for all peoples" (Isa. 25:6). God will be the chef—He'll prepare us a meal. In Heaven, God will overwhelm us with His humility and His grace.

BEING WITH GOD

Many books and programs these days talk about messages from the spirit realm, supposedly from people who have died and now speak through channelers or mediums. They claim to have come from Heaven to interact with loved ones, yet almost never do they talk about God or express wonder at seeing Jesus. But no one who had actually been in Heaven would neglect to mention what Scripture shows is the main focus. If you had spent an evening dining with a king, you wouldn't come back and talk about the place settings. When the Apostle John was shown Heaven and wrote about it to the church, he recorded the details—but first and foremost, from beginning to end, he kept talking about Jesus.

The presence of God is the essence of Heaven (just as the absence of God is the essence of hell). If we knew nothing more than that Heaven is God's dwelling place, it would be more than enough. The best part of life on the New Earth will be enjoying God's presence, having Him actually dwell among us (see Rev. 21:3-4). In the New Jerusalem, there will be no temple (v. 22). Everyone will be allowed unimpeded access into God's presence. "Blessed are those who ... may go through the gates into the city" (22:14).

What has God shown you today that makes you want to serve Him here and anticipate being with Him forever?

_____

_____

_____

_____

Heaven's greatest miracle will be our access to God. Today we may come to His throne spiritually through prayer. In the New Jerusalem, we will be able to come physically, through wide-open gates, to God's throne.

DAY 3

How Will We Worship God?

Has it happened to you—in prayer or corporate worship or during a walk on the beach—that for a few moments you experience the very presence of God? It's a tantalizing encounter, yet for most of us it tends to disappear quickly in the distractions of life. What will it be like to behold God's face and never be distracted by lesser things? What will it be like when every lesser thing points us back to God?

Many suppose beholding God would be of mere passing interest, becoming monotonous over time. But those who know God know He is anything but boring. Seeing God will be dynamic, not static. It will mean exploring new beauties, unfolding new mysteries—forever. We'll explore God's being, an experience delightful beyond comprehension.

The sense of wide-eyed wonder we see among Heaven's inhabitants in Revelation 4–5 suggests an ever-deepening appreciation of God's greatness. That isn't all there is to Heaven, but if it were, it would be more than enough. In Heaven we'll be at home with the God we love and who loves us wholeheartedly. Lovers don't bore each other. People who love God could never be bored in his presence.

ALL-ENCOMPASSING WORSHIP

Meeting God—when it truly happens—will be far more exhilarating than a great meal, hunting, gardening, mountain climbing, or watching the Super Bowl. Even if it were true (it isn't) that church services must be dull, there will be no church services in Heaven. The church (Christ's people) will be there. But there will be no temple, and as far as we know, no services (see Rev. 21:22).

Will we always be in engaged in worship? Yes and no. If we have a narrow view of worship, the answer is no. But if we have a broad view of worship, the answer is yes.

We won't always be on our faces at Christ's feet, worshiping Him, because Scripture says we'll be doing many other things—living in dwelling places, eating and drinking, reigning with Christ, and working for Him. Scripture depicts people standing, walking, traveling in and out of the city, and gathering at feasts. When doing these things, we won't be on our faces before Christ. Nevertheless, all that we do will be an act of worship. We'll enjoy full and unbroken fellowship with Christ. At times this will crescendo into greater heights of praise as we assemble with the multitudes who are also worshiping Him.

Worship involves more than singing and prayer. I often worship God while reading a book, riding a bike, or taking a walk. I'm worshiping Him now as I write. Yet too often I'm distracted and fail to acknowledge God along the way. In Heaven, God will always be first in my thinking.

Even now we're told, "Be joyful always; pray continually; give thanks in all circumstances" (1 Thess. 5:16-18). God expects us to do things such as work, rest, and be with our families, showing that we can be joyful, prayerful, and thankful while doing other things.

WHY WORSHIP CAN'T BE BORING

Some subjects become less interesting over time. Others become more fascinating. Nothing is more fascinating than God. The deeper we probe into His being, the more we want to know.

We'll never lose our fascination for God. As we get to know Him better. The thrill of knowing Him will never subside. The desire to know Him better will motivate everything we do.

To imagine that worshiping God could be boring is to impose on Heaven our bad experiences of so-called worship. Satan is determined to make church boring, and when it is, we assume Heaven will be also. But church can be exciting and worship exhilarating. That's what it will be in Heaven. We will see God and understand why the angels and other living creatures delight to worship Him.

We can never get enough of God. There's no end to what He knows, no end to what He can do, no end to who He is. He is mesmerizing to the depths of His being, and those depths will never be exhausted. No wonder those in Heaven always redirect their eyes to Him—they don't want to miss anything.

The world is full of praise-prompters—the New Earth will overflow with them. I've found great joy in moments where I've been lost in worship—often during church services—but they're too fleeting. If you've ever had a taste of true worship, you crave more of it, never less.

Has someone ever done something for you that made you so grateful you just can't stop saying thank you? If so, describe it.

_____

_____

_____

_____

This is how we should feel about God. In Heaven, worshiping God won't be restricted to a time on a sign, telling us when to start and stop. It will permeate our lives, energize our bodies, and fuel our imagination.

CHRIST AND HIS BRIDE

As the church, we're part of the ultimate Cinderella story—rescued from a home where we labor, often without appreciation or reward. One day we'll be taken into the arms of the Prince and whisked away to live in His palace. When "the wedding of the Lamb has come" (Rev. 19:7), the New Jerusalem, consisting not only of buildings but of God's people, will come down out of Heaven, "prepared as a bride beautifully dressed for her husband" (21:2). "And his bride has made herself ready. Fine linen, bright and clean, was given her to wear" (19:7-8). The eyes of the universe will be on the Bridegroom, but also on the bride for whom He died.

I have vivid memories of my daughters' pure beauty in their wedding dresses. The church, Christ's bride, should likewise be characterized by purity, as a fitting gift to our Bridegroom, the crown prince who has been utterly faithful to us.

If I were to ask you, "What does the fine linen the bride is wearing stand for?" you might be inclined to say, "The righteousness of Christ that covers us." Significantly, however, the text says something different: "Fine linen stands for the righteous acts of the saints" (v. 8).

Why do you suppose the fine linen is comprised of our acts?

_____

_____

The chosen princess, the church, can enter the presence of her Lord only because of the Bridegroom's work. Yet her wedding dress is woven through her many acts of faithfulness while away from her Bridegroom on the fallen earth.

The picture is compelling. Each prayer, each gift, each hour of fasting, each kindness to the needy, all of these are the threads that have been woven together into this wedding dress. Her works have been empowered by the Spirit, and she has spent her life on earth sewing her wedding dress for the day when she will be joined to her Beloved.

In what ways are you sewing your wedding garment?

_____

_____

_____

We have a wonderful reason to stay alive, though we are apart from our Beloved, because we aren't yet finished sewing our wedding dress. The wedding approaches, yet there's more for us to do to present ourselves pure before our Lord. We're eager for His return, but we don't sit idly by. Part of us wants fewer days between now and the wedding because we're so eager to be with our Beloved in our new home. But another part wants more days to better prepare for the wedding, to sew our dresses through acts of faithful service to God.

If the wedding of the Lamb were today, how would you feel about your preparedness?

❏ Uh oh. I haven't even started on my gown!

❏ I was supposed to be sewing a wedding garment?

❏ My gown isn't exactly fit for a royal wedding.

❏ I've given my best to making this gown. I can't wait for the Bridegroom to see it!

Write a prayer to your Bridegroom expressing whatever you are thinking about and feeling.

_____

_____

_____

_____

_____

_____

_____

DAY 4

Will We Actually Rule with Christ?

When Jesus was on trial, He said to Pilate, "My kingdom is not of this world. If it were, my servants would fight to prevent my arrest by the Jews. But now my kingdom is from another place. ... You are right in saying I am a king. In fact, for this reason I was born, and for this I came into the world" (John 18:36-37).

When Jesus said, "My kingdom is not of this world," He did not mean that His kingdom wouldn't be on this earth after it is transformed. He meant that His kingdom isn't of this earth as it is now, under the curse. Although Christ's kingdom isn't from the earth, it extends to the earth, and one day it will fully include the earth and be centered on it.

Read Zechariah 9:9-10 in the margin. When was the first portion of the prophecy fulfilled?
- ❏ the incarnation
- ❏ the triumphal entry
- ❏ the resurrection

When was/will the second part (be) fulfilled?

_____

_____

Matthew 21:5 makes it clear that Zechariah's prophecy concerns the Messiah. Just as the first part of the prophecy was literally fulfilled when Jesus rode a donkey into Jerusalem, we should expect that the second part will be literally fulfilled when Jesus brings peace to the nations and rules them all. Jesus will return to earth as "King of kings and Lord of lords" (Rev. 19:11-16). We're promised that "the LORD will be king over the whole earth" (Zech. 14:9).

> _"Rejoice greatly, O Daughter of Zion! Shout, Daughter of Jerusalem! See, your king comes to you, righteous and having salvation, gentle and riding on a donkey, on a colt, the foal of a donkey. I will take away the chariots from Ephraim and the war-horses from Jerusalem, and the battle bow will be broken. He will proclaim peace to the nations. His rule will extend from sea to sea and from the River to the ends of the earth."_
>
> ZECHARIAH 9:9-10

God created Adam and Eve to be king and queen over the earth. Their job was to rule the earth, to the glory of God.

They failed.

Jesus Christ is the last Adam, and the church is His bride, the last Eve. Christ is King, the church is His queen. Christ will exercise dominion over all nations of the earth: "He will rule from sea to sea and from the River to the ends of the earth. ... All kings will bow down to him and all nations will serve him" (Ps. 72:8,11). As the new head of the human race, Christ—with His beloved people as His bride and co-rulers—will at last accomplish what was entrusted to Adam and Eve. God's saints will fulfill on the New Earth the role God first assigned to Adam and Eve on the old earth.

Prior to Christ's return, His kingdom will be intermingled with the world's cultures (see Matt. 13:24-30). But His followers will be growing in character and proving their readiness to rule.

What experience have you had lately that Christ either has used or could use to prepare you to rule with Him? (Don't overlook critical character traits such as humility.)

_____

_____

_____

Through adversity and opportunity, as well as in their artistic and cultural accomplishments, believers will be groomed for their leadership roles in Christ's eternal earthly kingdom. Their society-transforming creative skills will be put on prominent display in the new universe, where they will "shine like the sun in the kingdom of their Father" (Matt. 13:43).

WHY ARE WE SURPRISED THAT WE'LL RULE THE EARTH?

Often Christians are surprised to learn that we will reign in eternity over lands, cities, and nations. Many are skeptical—it's a foreign concept that seems fanciful. Nothing demonstrates how far we've distanced ourselves from our biblical calling like our lack of knowledge about our destiny to rule the earth. Why are we so surprised, when it is spoken of throughout the Old Testament and repeatedly reaffirmed in the New Testament?

Paul addressed the subject of Christians ruling as if it were Theology 101: "Do you not know that the saints will judge the world? ... Do you not know that we will judge angels?" (1 Cor. 6:2-3). The form of the verb in this question implies that we won't simply judge them a single time but will continually rule them. If Paul spoke of this future reality as if it were something every child should know, why is it so foreign to Christians today?

Why do you think many of us are surprised by this teaching?

_____

_____

_____

Since mankind's reign on the earth is introduced in the first chapters of the Bible, mentioned throughout the Old Testament, discussed by Jesus in the Gospels, by Paul in the Epistles, and repeated by John in Revelation, it is remarkable that we would fail to see it.

OUR INHERITANCE: OWNING AND RULING THE LAND

Currently, on this earth under the curse, we serve Christ and share in His sufferings because the earth is under siege. It's being claimed by a false king, Satan, and his false princes, the fallen angels. It's being claimed by human kings, rebels who set themselves up against God and violate His standards by declaring their independence from Him.

Those who are co-heirs with Christ engage in spiritual warfare to reclaim the hearts of mankind for God's glory. After the final battle is won by Christ, we will rule the earth with Him as co-heirs of His kingdom.

The government of the New Earth won't be a democracy. It won't be majority rule, and it won't be driven by opinion polls. Instead, every citizen of Heaven will have an appointed role, one that fulfills him or her and contributes to the whole. No one will "fall through the cracks" in God's kingdom. No one will feel worthless or insignificant.

"For everyone who exalts himself will be humbled, and the one who humbles himself will be exalted." LUKE 14:11

A hierarchy of government will exist, but there's no indication of a relational hierarchy. There will be no pride, envy, boasting, or anything sin related. Our differences will be a manifestation of God's creativity. As we're different in race, nationality, gender, personality, gifting, and passions, so we'll be different in positions of service.

All of us will have some responsibility in which we serve God. Scripture teaches that our service for Him now on earth will be evaluated to help determine how we'll serve him on the New Earth.

What does Luke 14:11 tell you about leadership positions on the New Earth? _____

_____

_____

The humble servant will be put in charge of much, whereas the one who lords it over others will have power taken away. If we serve faithfully on the present earth, God will give us permanent management positions on the New Earth. "Whoever can be trusted with very little can also be trusted with much" (Luke 16:10). The Owner has His eye on us—if we prove faithful, He'll be pleased to entrust more to us.

Imagine responsibility, service, and leadership that's pure joy. The fear, anxiety, dread, and turmoil we associate with certain activities on the present earth will be gone. Our service will not only bring Him glory but will also bring us joy.

LOOKING FORWARD TO WHAT GOD HAS FOR US

The Master will say, "Well done, good and faithful servant! You have been faithful with a few things; I will put you in charge of many things. Come and share your master's happiness!" (Matt. 25:23).

Entering the Master's joy means our Master Himself is joyful. He takes joy in Himself, in His children, and in His creation. His joy is contagious. Once we're liberated from the sin that blocks us from God's joy and our own, we'll enter into His joy. Joy will be the very air we breathe. The Lord is inexhaustible—therefore His joy is inexhaustible.

Describe a time from your childhood when you felt good about something you accomplished.

_____

_____

Did anyone affirm your work? ❏ yes ❏ no ❏ I don't remember

If so, how did that affirmation feel? If not, how do you think affirmation would have felt?

_____

_____

_____

God is grooming us for leadership. He's watching to see how we demonstrate our faithfulness. He does that through His apprenticeship program that prepares us for Heaven. Christ is not simply preparing a place for us; He is preparing us for that place.

We all have dreams but often don't see them realized. We become discouraged and lose hope. But as Christ's apprentices, we must learn certain disciplines.

Apprentices must work and study hard to prepare for the next test or challenge. They may wish for three weeks of vacation or more pay, but the Master may know these would not lead to success. He may override His apprentices' desires so that they might learn perspective and patience, which will serve them well in the future. While the young apprentices experience the death of their dreams, the Master is shaping them to dream greater dreams that they will one day live out on the New Earth with enhanced wisdom, skill, appreciation, and joy.

Through the challenges you now face, what dreams might God be preparing you to live out on the New Earth?

_____

_____

_____

_____

DAY 5

How Will We Rule God's Kingdom?

The world as it was and as it will be is exceedingly good. The world *as it is now*, inhabited by humanity, is twisted. But this is a temporary condition with an eternal remedy: Christ's redemptive work. We need to think carefully when we read Scriptures that talk about "the world." I recommend adding the words *as it is now, under the curse* to keep the biblical distinctions clear in our minds.

In the passages below, add the distinction "as it is now, under the curse, after the word "world."

"Friendship with the world _____

_____ is hatred toward God" (Jas. 4:4)

.

"Do not be conformed to this world _____

_____ " (Rom. 12:2, NKJV).

Paul said that Christ "gave himself for our sins to rescue us from the present evil age" (Gal. 1:4). Not all worlds and all ages are evil, but only this world in this present age. When Jesus called Satan "the prince of this world" (John 14:30; 16:11) and Paul called Satan "the god of this age" (2 Cor. 4:4), it was a relative and temporary designation. God is still God over the universe, still sovereign over earth and over Satan. But the Devil is the usurper who has tried to steal earth's throne. In His time, God will take back the throne, as the God-man Jesus Christ, at last restoring and raising earth.

Paul encouraged us not to become engrossed in the world as it is because "this world in its present form is passing away" (1 Cor. 7:31). God will not bring an end to the earth; rather, He will bring this temporary rebellion to an end. He will transform earth into a realm of unsurpassed magnificence, for His glory and for our good.

WHAT WE KNOW ABOUT GOD'S KINGDOM ... AND OURS

In Daniel 7 we're given a prophetic vision of four earthly kingdoms, beginning with Nebuchadnezzar's Babylon, that will one day be forever replaced by a fifth kingdom (Dan. 7:13-14). The Messiah's dominion—in context, a kingdom on earth—will be "everlasting" and "will not pass away" and "will never be destroyed" (v. 14). Christ will not merely destroy the earth where fallen kings once ruled. Rather, He will rule over the same earth, transformed and new.

At Daniel's request, an angel provided an interpretation of his vision: "The four great beasts are four kingdoms that will rise from the earth" (v. 17). Then the angel made an extraordinary statement: "But the saints of the Most High will receive the kingdom and will possess it forever—yes, for ever and ever" (v. 18). This statement makes clear both the kingdom's location (earth) and its duration (eternal).

The ongoing succession of earth's unrighteous rulers should make us hunger for the day when our righteous God will rule, not just in Heaven but on earth. At stake is whether God's will shall be done on earth. The answer is that it will be done on earth, for all eternity, under the reign of Christ and redeemed mankind, His servant kings.

God has never abandoned His original plan that righteous human beings will inhabit and rule the earth. That's not merely an argument from silence. Daniel 7:18 explicitly reveals that "the saints of the Most High will receive the kingdom and will possess it forever."

God intended for humans to occupy the whole earth and reign over it. This dominion would produce God-exalting societies in which we would exercise the creativity, imagination, intellect, and skills befitting beings created in God's image, thereby manifesting His attributes. As God's subcreators, we should together make the invisible God visible, thus glorifying Him in the sight of all creation.

In the paragraph above, circle the phrase you think best defines what it means to glorify God.

This reigning, expanding, culture-enriching purpose of God for mankind on earth was never revoked or abandoned. It has only been interrupted and twisted by the fall. But neither Satan nor sin are able to thwart God's purposes. Christ's redemptive work will ultimately restore, enhance, and expand God's original plan. You could have circled "manifesting His attributes" or, my preference, "making the invisible God visible." Either of those statements defines what the Bible means to glorify God.

Describe a time when someone "made the invisible God visible" for you. _____

_____

_____

What would you like to say to that person? _____

_____

_____

Daniel 7:21-22 says an earthly ruler "was waging war against the saints and defeating them, until the Ancient of Days came and pronounced judgment in favor of the saints of the Most High, and the time came when they possessed the kingdom."

THE KINGDOM TRANSFER

I believe the "greatness of the kingdoms under the whole heaven" (Dan. 7: 27) that will be "handed over to the saints" includes all that makes the nations great. That would include, among other things, their cultural, artistic, athletic, scientific, and intellectual achievements. All of these will not be lost or destroyed but "handed over to the saints" as they rule God's eternal kingdom on the New Earth. We will become the stewards, the managers of the world's wealth and accomplishments.

Consider the marvels of this revelation. God's children who suffered under ungodly earthly kings will forever take their place as earthly kings. The great cultural accomplishments of ungodly nations will be handed over to God's people to manage and (I assume) develop and expand.

The very earth to which Satan once laid claim will be stripped from his grasp and given to those he hates and seeks to destroy—God's saints. Notice it doesn't say that the earth's kingdoms will be destroyed but that they will be "handed over" to the saints, placed under their just rule. All the wrongs done on earth by tyrants will be a thing of the past. No more persecution and injustice. The earth that was first put under mankind's dominion and was twisted by the fall will be redeemed, restored, and put under the righteous rule of a redeemed and restored mankind.

As we've seen from Isaiah 60 and Revelation 21, there will still be nations on the New Earth, and they will still have rulers. But they will be righteous rulers, subordinate to Christ. People of every national and ethnic group will worship the Lamb. Some will rule over cities; others will rule over nations.

SERVICE AS A REWARD

Jesus said, "Rejoice and be glad, because great is your reward in heaven" (Matt. 5:12). Should we be excited that God will reward us by making us rulers in His kingdom? Absolutely. Service is a reward, not a punishment. This idea is foreign to people who dislike their work and only put up with it until retirement.

We think that faithful work should be rewarded by a vacation for the rest of our lives. But God offers us something very different: more work, more responsibilities, increased opportunities, along with greater abilities, resources, wisdom, and empowerment. We will have sharp minds, strong bodies, clear purpose, and unabated joy. The more we serve Christ now, the greater our capacity will be to serve Him in Heaven.

Will everyone be given the opportunity to rule in the new universe? The Apostle Paul said that eternal rewards are available "not only to me, but also to all who have longed for his appearing" (2 Tim. 4:8). The word "all" is encouraging. "The Lord will reward everyone for whatever good he does" (Eph. 6:8). It won't be just a select few rewarded with positions of leadership. God will choose who reigns as kings, and I think some great surprises are in store for us. Christ gives us clues in Scripture as to the type of person He will choose.

According to the following Scriptures, who will inherit or possess the Kingdom?

Matthew 5:3 _____

Matthew 5:5 _____

Matthew 5:10 _____

1 Peter 5:5-6 _____

Think of someone you know who fits those criteria. Which qualities do you think will make him or her a great ruler?

_____

_____

Look around you to see the meek and the humble. They may include street sweepers, locksmith's assistants, bus drivers, or stay-at-home moms who spend their days changing diapers, doing laundry, packing lunches, drying tears, and driving carpools for God.

I once gave one of my books to a delightful hotel bellman. I discovered he was a committed Christian. He said he'd been praying for our group, which was holding a conference at the hotel. Later I gave him a little gift. He seemed stunned, overwhelmed. With tears in his eyes he said, "You didn't need to do that. I'm only a bellman." The moment he said it, I realized that this brother had spent his life serving. It will likely be someone like him that I'll have the privilege of serving under in God's kingdom. He was "only a bellman" who spoke with warmth and love, who served, who quietly prayed in the background for the success of a conference in his hotel. I saw Jesus in that bellman, and there was no "only" about him.

Who will be the kings of the New Earth? I think that bellman will be one of them. And I'll be honored to carry his bags.

---

1. Augustine, *City of God,* 22, 30 and *Confessions* 1, 1, quoted in John E. Rotelle, *Augustine Day by Day* (New York: Catholic Book Publishing, 1986).
2. Steven J. Lawson, *Heaven Help Us!* (Colorado Springs: NavPress, 1995), 142.
3. John Piper, *Desiring God: Meditations of a Christian Hedonist* (Sisters, OR: Multnomah, 1996), 50.

What Will Our Lives Be Like in Heaven?

DAY 1

Should We Expect to Maintain Our Own Identities?

A man wrote me expressing his fear of losing his identity in Heaven. He was afraid that we'd all be alike, that he and his treasured friends would lose their distinguishing traits and eccentricities that make them special. But he needn't worry. We can all be like Jesus in character yet very different in personality.

Individual identity is an essential aspect of personhood. God is the Creator of individual identities and personalities. He makes no two snowflakes, much less two people, alike. Not even identical twins are identical. Individuality preceded sin and the curse. Individuality was God's plan from the beginning.

According to Luke 15:4-7, 10, who do Heaven's inhabitants rejoice over coming to God?

❑ nameless multitudes   ❑ each and every person

That's a powerful affirmation of Heaven's view of each individual. When Moses and Elijah appeared at Christ's transfiguration, the disciples recognized them as the distinct individuals they were. When we sit at a banquet and eat with Abraham, Isaac, and others, we will be sitting with particular individuals (see Matt. 8:11).

Beside the next several paragraphs, jot notes in the margin of reasons to believe you will retain your individuality in Heaven.

You will be you in Heaven. Who else would you be? If Bob, a man on earth, is no longer Bob when he gets to Heaven, then, in fact, Bob did not go to Heaven. If when I arrive in Heaven I'm not the same person with the same identity, history, and memory, then I didn't go to Heaven.

"It is I myself!"

LUKE 24:39

      The resurrected Jesus did not become someone else; He remained who He was before His resurrection (see Luke 24:39). In John's Gospel, Jesus dealt with Mary, Thomas, and Peter in very personal ways, drawing on His previous knowledge of them (see John 20:10-18,24-29; 21:15-22). His knowledge and relationships from His preresurrected state carried over. When Thomas said, "My Lord and my God" (20:28), he knew he was speaking to the same Jesus he'd followed. When John said, "It is the Lord!" he meant, "It's really him—the Jesus we have known" (21:4-7).

      If we aren't ourselves in the afterlife, then we can't be held accountable for what we did in this life. The judgment would be meaningless. If Barbara is no longer Barbara, she can't be rewarded or held accountable for anything Barbara did. Judgment and eternal rewards depend on people's retaining their distinct identities from this life to the next.

      Some read "participate in the divine nature" (2 Pet. 1:4) and imagine we will all become indistinguishable from God. But to imagine we'll lose our personal identities is a Hindu belief, not a Christian belief. The verse in 2 Peter means we're covered with Christ's righteousness. We'll participate in God's holiness yet fully retain our God-crafted individuality.

What do you think is the strongest reason to believe you will retain your individuality in Heaven?

_____

List three distinct characteristics that make you who you are.

1. _____

2. _____

3. _____

You are your memory, personality traits, gifts, passions, preferences, and interests. In the final resurrection I believe all of these facets will be restored and amplified, untarnished by sin and the curse.

Describe a time you really felt good about yourself, not in pride or arrogance, but when you sensed you honored God, helped the needy, were faithful, humble, and had a servant heart.

_____

_____

Did you name a time you encouraged someone? When you experienced who you were meant to be? When you were running or working and felt you were strong enough to go on forever—though later you could hardly get out of bed? That was a little taste of who you'll be in Heaven.

We have become sinful versions of what God intended. Our deceitfulness, laziness, lust, deafness, disability, and disease is not the real us. They are temporary perversions that will be eliminated. They're the cancer that the Great Physician will surgically remove. His redemptive work means never again will they return.

When you're on the New Earth, for the first time you'll be the person God created you to be.

WILL WE BECOME ANGELS?

I'm often asked if people, particularly children, become angels when they die. The answer is no. Death is a relocation of the same person from one place to another. The place changes, but the person remains the same. The same person who becomes absent from his or her body becomes present with the Lord (see 2 Cor. 5:8).

Angels are angels. Humans are humans. Angels are beings with their own histories and memories, with distinct identities, reflected in the fact that they have personal names, such as Michael and Gabriel. Under God's direction, they serve us on earth (Heb. 1:14). In Heaven human beings will govern angels (1 Cor. 6:2-3).

The fact that angels have served us on earth will make meeting them in Heaven particularly fascinating. They've been with us from childhood, protecting us, standing by us, doing whatever they could on our behalf (Matt. 18:10). They may have witnessed virtually every moment of our lives. Besides God Himself, no one could know us better.

If we really believed angels were with us daily, here and now, how might it motivate us to make wiser choices?

_____

_____

What will it be like not only to have them show us around the present Heaven but also to walk and talk with them on the New Earth? What stories will they tell us, including what really happened that day at the lake 35 years ago when we almost drowned? They've guarded us, gone to fierce battle for us, served as God's agents in answering prayers. How great it will be to get to know these brilliant ancient creatures who have lived with God from their creation! We'll consult them as well as advise them, realizing they too can learn from us, God's image-bearers.

IN HEAVEN WILL WE BE CALLED BY OUR PRESENT NAMES?

The names of God's children appear in the Lamb's book of life (Rev. 20:15; 21:27). I believe those are our earthly names, given by our parents. God calls people in Heaven by those same names—Abraham, Isaac, and Jacob, for instance. The names of the 12 sons of Israel and of the apostles, are written on the city's gates and the foundations of its walls (see Rev. 21:12-14). Our names reflect our individuality. To have the same name written in Heaven that was ours on earth speaks of the continuity between this life and the next.

In addition to our earthly names, we'll receive new names in Heaven (Isa. 62:2; 65:15; Rev. 2:17; 3:12). New names don't invalidate the old ones. Many people had multiple names in Scripture: Jacob was also Israel; Cephas was also Peter; Saul was also Paul.

WILL WE REALLY BE PERFECT?

In Heaven we'll be perfectly human. Adam and Eve were perfectly human until they bent themselves into sinners. Then they lost something that was an original part of their humanity—moral perfection. Since then, under sin's curse, we've been human but never perfectly human.

Dream a moment. To what aspect of being totally free from sin's curse do you most look forward?

_____

_____

We've always carried sin's baggage. What relief it will be not to have to guard our eyes and our minds! We will not need to defend against pride and lust because there will be none. In Heaven we won't just be better than we are now—we'll be better than Adam and Eve were before they fell. We'll be a redeemed humanity with knowledge of God, including His grace, far exceeding theirs.

In Heaven we'll be perfectly human, but we'll still be finite. Our bodies will be perfect in that they won't be diseased or crippled. But that doesn't mean they won't have limits. We often misuse the term _perfect_ when it describes our state in Heaven. I've heard it said, for instance, "We'll communicate perfectly, so we'll never be at a loss for words."

I disagree. I expect we'll sometimes grasp for words to describe the wondrous things we'll experience. I expect I'll stand in speechless wonder at the glory of God. I'll be morally perfect, but that doesn't mean I'll be capable of doing anything. (Adam and Eve were morally perfect, but that didn't mean they could automatically invent nuclear submarines or defy gravity. They were perfect yet finite, just as we will be.)

Someone asked me, "If we're sinless, will we still be human?" Although sin is part of us now, it's not essential to our humanity—in fact, it's foreign to it. It's what twists us and keeps us from being what we once were—and one day will be.

Our greatest deliverance in Heaven will be from ourselves. Our deceit, corruption, self-righteousness, self-sufficiency, hypocrisy—all will be forever gone. In liberating us from sin and all its consequences, the resurrection will free us to live with God, gaze on Him, and enjoy His uninterrupted fellowship forever, with no threat that anything will ever again come between us and Him.

DAY 2

What Will Our Bodies Be Like?

As we discussed in week 3, our resurrected bodies will be real physical bodies, just as Christ's was and is. But what will our bodies look like? How will they function?

Our resurrection bodies will be free of the curse of sin, redeemed, and restored to their original beauty and purpose that goes back to Eden. The only bodies we've ever known are weak and diseased remnants of the original bodies God made for humans. But the bodies we'll have on the New Earth, in our resurrection, will be even more glorious than those of Adam and Eve.

WILL OUR RESURRECTION BODIES HAVE FIVE SENSES?

God designed us with five senses. They're part of what makes us human. Our resurrection bodies will surely have these senses. I expect they will increase in their power and sensitivity.

Do your senses currently suffer any of the following?

❏ eyes that require correction   ❏ hearing loss

❏ sense of smell less than perfect   ❏ touch less sensitive

❏ less acute taste

How have these limitations affected you?

_____

_____

How do you imagine food will taste or flowers smell with senses sharper than you've ever experienced?

_____

_____

We'll see the New Earth, feel it, smell it, taste its fruits, and hear its sounds. Not figuratively. Literally. We know this because we're promised resurrection bodies like Christ's. He saw, heard, felt, cooked, and ate. Heaven's delights will stretch our glorified senses to their limits.

It seems reasonable to suggest our resurrected senses will function at levels we've never known. David prayed, "I praise you because I am fearfully and wonderfully made" (Ps. 139:14). How much more will we praise God for the wonders of our resurrection bodies?

Scripture speaks repeatedly about eating in Heaven. What will our resurrected taste buds be able to taste? The best food here on earth is tainted by the curse. Our taste buds at their best are still defective. Think of the best meal you've ever eaten, the best dessert you've ever tasted. As good as those were, they were just a hint of what's to come—a good enough hint to make us long for Heaven.

Describe in detail your favorite meal: appetizers, entrees, dessert, drink. Order as if you were selecting from the menu of the finest restaurant. _____

_____

_____

Now imagine the server offers you something new, so mouth-watering that you forget the meal you ordered. How do you feel?

❏ disappointed   ❏ delighted   ❏ excited

❏ amazed   ❏ other _____

To be restored to the sensory abilities of Adam and Eve would be thrilling enough. But it seems likely our resurrected bodies will surpass theirs. What God remakes, He only improves. On the New Earth I think we'll continually be discovering, to our delight, what we never knew existed, what we've been missing all our lives. No joy is greater than the joy of discovery. The God who always surpasses our expectations will always give us more of Himself and His creation to discover.

WILL WE EXPERIENCE HUNGER, AND WILL WE DIGEST FOOD?

Will we get hungry on the New Earth? Some people say no because "Never again will they hunger; never again will they thirst" (Rev. 7:16). But this doesn't mean that we'll lack an appetite or desire; it means our desires will be met. We will never go hungry or go thirsty. To find pleasure in eating assumes we desire to eat. Hunger and thirst are good things (if food and drink are freely available), and God assures us that on the New Earth they always will be.

What does Revelation 7:16 suggest about thirst on the New Earth?

_____

_____

God doesn't say we won't need to drink. Rather, he says he will lead us to drink. The natural stimulus to motivate drinking is thirst. We will presumably thirst for water, as we will thirst for God. But our thirst will never go unsatisfied.

Paul quoted the Corinthians: "You say, 'Food is for the stomach, and the stomach is for food.' This is true, though someday God will do away with both of them" (1 Cor. 6:13, NLT). Some people think God was saying here that we won't eat and won't have stomachs or digestive systems.

But in context Paul was simply saying that the old body will die, so we shouldn't let the desires of that body control us.

Some people argue that we won't eat or drink in Heaven because they're aghast at the thought of digestion and elimination. Could God make it so our new bodies wouldn't go through the same digestive and elimination processes they do now? Certainly. Will He? We don't know. But no aspect of our God-created physiology can be bad. To imagine otherwise is christoplatonism again. Did Adam and Eve experience digestion and elimination in a perfect world? Of course. Jesus never sinned, but His body functioned just as ours do.

WILL WE BE MALE OR FEMALE?

One book about Heaven claims, "There will be no male and female human beings. We shall all be children of God and sex will be no part of our nature."[1] The same book says, "Men will no longer be men nor will women be women."[2]

Similarly, another book says of those in Heaven, "They have reached that androgynous condition in which sex distinctions are transcended, or rather, in which the qualities of both sexes are blended together."[3]

Some people try to prove there will be no gender in Heaven by citing Paul's statement that in Christ there is neither "male nor female" (Gal. 3:28).

How could someone argue from Galatians 3:28 that Heaven's inhabitants are without gender?

_____

_____

Read Galatians 3:25-29. When you read this passage in context, what does it teach?
- ❏ no gender in heaven
- ❏ salvation available to all
- ❏ no gender in the church

Paul referred to something that's already true on earth: the equality of men and women in Christ. The issue isn't the obliteration of sexuality (you don't lose your gender at conversion). The issue is salvation freely available regardless of gender.

Was Jesus genderless after His resurrection? Of course not. No one mistook Him for a woman—or as androgynous. We'll never be genderless because human bodies aren't genderless. The point of the resurrection is that we will have real human bodies essentially linked to our original ones. Gender is a God-created aspect of humanity.

In my novel *Deadline*, Finney addresses this matter with his angel:

"But I am still a man here, and everyone I see is clearly male or female, more distinctly in fact than on earth. I had thought perhaps there would be no gender here. I had read that we would all be ... like angels, like you."

Zyor looked surprised.

"You are like us in that you do not marry and bear children here. But as for your being a man, what else would you be? Elyon may unmake what men make, but he does not unmake what he makes. He made you male, as he made your mother and wife and daughters female. Gender is not merely a component of your being to be added in or extracted and discarded. It is an essential part of who you are."[4]

WILL WE WEAR CLOTHES?

Because Adam and Eve were naked and unashamed, some argue that in Heaven we won't need to wear clothes. But even in the present Heaven, before the final resurrection, people are depicted as wearing clothes, white robes that depict our righteousness in Christ (see Rev. 3:4; 6:11). It appears we'll wear clothes—not because there will be shame or temptation but perhaps because they will enhance our appearance and comfort.

Wearing robes might strike us as foreign or formal. But to first-century readers, anything but robes would have seemed strange because robes were what they normally wore. Rather than conclude that we'll all wear robes, a better deduction is that we'll all dress normally, as we did on the old earth.

Which aspect of having an improved, resurrected body most appeals to you?

- ❏ smooth, restored skin
- ❏ keener senses
- ❏ clear, healthy lungs
- ❏ stronger muscles
- ❏ healthy bones and joints
- ❏ other_____

Why? _____

_____

_____

DAY 3

What Will a Typical Day Be Like?

Some people have asked "Will we rest in Heaven?" I respond that when God created the world, He rested on the seventh day (Gen. 2:2). God set aside days and weeks of rest, and He even rested the earth itself every seventh year (see Lev. 25:4-5). This is the rest we can anticipate on the New Earth—times of joyful praise and relaxed fellowship.

Our lives in Heaven will include rest (see Heb. 4:1-11). What feels better than putting your head on the pillow after a hard day's work? It's good to sit back and have a glass of iced tea, feel the sun on your face, or to have nothing to do but read a good book or take your dog for a walk and tell God how grateful you are for His kindness. Rest is good. So good that God built it into His creation and into His law.

We catch glimpses of enjoying both work and rest at once. I used to feel this when body, mind, and the beauty around me sometimes "kicked in" on a 10-mile run. I've experienced the same bicycling, when I've felt I could ride forever and the peddling I was doing was part of a great rest. I can be working intently at something I love yet find the work restful and refreshing.

"Blessed are the dead who die in the Lord from now on.' 'Yes,' says the Spirit, 'they will rest from their labor, for their deeds will follow them.'"

REVELATION 14:13

What do you love to do under the category of active rest?

_____

_____

WILL WE SLEEP?

Some people argue that we won't sleep because we'll have perfect bodies. But the same argument would apply to eating—yet we know we'll eat. Adam and Eve were created perfect, but did they sleep? Probably. If so, sleep cannot be an imperfection. It's a matter of God's design for the rhythm of life.

Sleep is one of life's great pleasures. It's part of God's perfect plan for humans in bodies living on the earth. Troubled sleep and sleeplessness are products of sin and the curse, but sleep itself is God's gift. I believe we will both need it and enjoy it.

Some people say, "But there won't be fatigue." Why not? Couldn't resources be depleted and renewed in a perfect but finite world, just as they were in Eden? We'll rest and be refreshed in Heaven.

WILL WE WORK?

The idea of working in Heaven is foreign to many people. Yet Scripture clearly teaches it. Work was part of the original Eden. It was part of a perfect human life on Earth. Work wasn't part of the curse. The curse, rather, made work menial, tedious, and frustrating. On the New Earth work will be redeemed and transformed into what God intended.

In the margin, underline the active verb in Revelation 22:3.

What do John 4:34 and 5:17 suggest about being like the Father and Jesus? _____

_____

Serve is a verb. Servants are people who are active and occupied as they carry out tasks. We'll have work to do, satisfying and enriching work that we can't wait to get back to, work that'll never be drudgery. God is the primary worker, and as His image-bearers, we're made to work.

> *"There will no longer be any curse. The throne of God and of the Lamb will be in the city, and His servants will serve Him."*
>
> REVELATION 2:3, HCSB

Since work began before sin and the curse, and since God, who is without sin, is a worker, we should assume human beings will work on the New Earth. We should assume we'll be able to resume the work started by Adam and Eve, exercising godly dominion over the earth, ruling it for God's glory.

But we don't need to just assume this. Scripture directly tells us. When the faithful servant enters Heaven, he is not offered retirement.

What are the faithful offered according to Matthew 25:23?

_____

_____

To what does "the joy of your Lord" seem to be connected?
- ❑ becoming king of the world
- ❑ becoming a servant
- ❑ becoming ruler over many things

What kind of work will we do in Heaven? Maybe you'll build a cabinet with Joseph of Nazareth. Or with Jesus. Maybe you'll tend sheep with David, discuss medicine with Luke, sew with Dorcas, make clothes with Lydia, design a new tent with Paul or Priscilla, write a song with Isaac Watts, ride horses with John Wesley, or sing with Keith Green. Maybe you'll write a theology of the Trinity, bouncing your thoughts off Paul, John, Polycarp, Cyprian, Augustine, Calvin, Wesley ... and even Jesus.

Our work will be joyful and fulfilling, giving glory to God. What could be better? Generally, unemployed people aren't happy. Work's a blessing and not just because of its financial rewards. Even in a world under the curse, most of us have known satisfaction in our work.

Jesus said to His Father, "I brought glory to you here on earth by doing everything you told me to do" (John 17:4, NLT). How will we glorify God for eternity? By doing everything He tells us to do. What did God first tell mankind to do? Fill the earth and exercise dominion over it. What will we do for eternity to glorify God? Exercise dominion over the earth, demonstrating God's creativity and ingenuity as His image-bearers, producing Christ-exalting culture.

What can you do today to promote a Christ-exalting culture?

_____

_____

_____

_____

DAY 4

What Will Our
Relationships Be Like?

Through the ages Christians have anticipated eternal reunion with their loved ones, but many people minimize human relationships in Heaven. Protestant reformer John Calvin said, "To be in Paradise and live with God is not to speak to each other and be heard by each other, but is only to enjoy God, to feel his good will, and rest in him."[5]

To Calvin's credit, he longed for the joy to be found in God. But he imagined a false dichotomy between the joys of relating to God and relating to God's children.

To take pleasure in another image-bearer doesn't offend God; it pleases him. To enjoy a conversation with a brother or sister does not require making that person an idol or competitor with God. God was supremely pleased that Adam and Eve enjoyed each other's company in Paradise. God is our father, and fathers delight in their children's close relationships.

Describe a time when sharing a joy made it greater for you.

_____

_____

Why did the other person's joy add to your own?

_____

_____

Some people falsely assume that when we give attention to people, it automatically distracts us from God. But even now, in a fallen world, people can turn my attention toward God. In Heaven, no person will distract us from God. We will never experience any conflict between worshiping God Himself and enjoying God's people. Deep and satisfying human relationships will be among God's greatest gifts.

WHAT DID PAUL SAY ABOUT REUNION IN HEAVEN?

Paul told the Thessalonians we'll be reunited with believing family and friends in Heaven: "God will bring with Jesus those who have fallen asleep in him. ... We who are still alive and are left will be caught up together with them. ... And so we will be with the Lord forever" (1 Thess. 4:14,17). Our source of comfort isn't only that we'll be with the Lord in Heaven but also that we'll be with each other.

Name some people you long to see in Heaven and describe why.

1. from your family _____

_____

2. someone you want to thank _____

_____

3. someone who helped lead you to know Christ _____

_____

Puritan Richard Baxter wrote: "I know that Christ is all in all; and that it is the presence of God that makes Heaven to be heaven. But yet it much sweetens the thoughts of that place to me that there are there such a multitude of my most dear and precious friends in Christ."[6]

WILL WE RECOGNIZE EACH OTHER?

Asked if we would recognize friends in Heaven, George MacDonald responded, "Shall we be greater fools in Paradise than we are here?"[7] Yet many people wonder whether we'll know each other in Heaven. The question is based on the false assumption that we'll be disembodied spirits who lose our identities and memories.

Christ's disciples recognized Him countless times after His resurrection. They recognized Him on the shore as He cooked breakfast for them (see John 21:1-14). They recognized Him when He appeared to a skeptical Thomas (see John 20:24-29). They recognized Him when He appeared to five hundred people at once (see 1 Cor. 15:6).

But what about Mary at the garden tomb or the two men on the road to Emmaus? They didn't recognize Jesus. Some people have argued from this that Jesus was unrecognizable. But a closer look shows otherwise.

Read John 20:15-16 carefully. What happened when Mary really looked at the resurrected Jesus?

❏ He disappeared out of her sight.

❏ His identity was hidden from her eyes.

❏ She recognized Him.

Read Luke 24:15-16. Why did the disciples on Emmaus road not recognize Jesus? _____

_____

At Christ's transfiguration, Christ's disciples recognized Moses and Elijah, even though they couldn't have known what the two men looked like. This may suggest that personality will emanate through a person's body so that we'll instantly recognize people we know of but haven't previously met. If we can recognize those we've never seen, how much more will we recognize our family and friends?

The continuity of our resurrection minds and bodies argues that we'll have no trouble recognizing each other—in fact, we'll have much less trouble. In Heaven we probably won't fail to recognize an acquaintance in a crowd or to remember people's names.

WILL THERE BE MARRIAGE, FAMILIES, AND FRIENDSHIPS?

One group of religious leaders, the Sadducees, tried to trick Jesus with a question about marriage in Heaven. They didn't believe in the resurrection of the dead. Attempting to make Him look foolish, they told Jesus of a woman who had seven husbands who all died. They asked Him, "Now then, at the resurrection, whose wife will she be of the seven, since all of them were married to her?" (Matt. 22:28).

Christ replied, "At the resurrection people will neither marry nor be given in marriage; they will be like the angels in heaven" (v. 30).

Many people experience a great deal of regret and misunderstanding about this passage. A woman wrote me, "I struggle with the idea that there won't be marriage in heaven. I believe I'll really miss it."

But the Bible does not teach there will be no marriage in Heaven. In fact, it makes clear there will be marriage in Heaven. What it says is we'll all be part of one marriage, between Christ and His bride.

The one-flesh marital union we know on earth is a signpost pointing to our relationship with Christ. Once we reach the destination, the signpost becomes unnecessary. That one marriage—our marriage to Christ—will be so completely satisfying that even the most wonderful earthly marriage couldn't be as fulfilling. All the human marriages that pointed to the ultimate marriage will have served their noble purpose and will be assimilated into the one great marriage they foreshadowed.

In the next two paragraphs underline phrases that describe our relationships with husbands/wives from this life.

We long for a perfect marriage, and that's exactly what we'll have— a perfect marriage with Christ. My wife, Nanci, is my best friend and my closest sister in Christ. Will we become more distant in the new world? Of course not—we'll become closer, I'm convinced. The God who said "It is not good for the man to be alone" (Gen. 2:18) is the giver and blesser of our relationships. Life on this earth matters. What we do here touches strings that reverberate for all eternity. Nothing will take away from the fact that Nanci and I are marriage partners here and that we invest so much of our lives in each other, serving Christ together. I fully expect no one besides God will understand me better on the New Earth, and there's nobody whose company I'll seek and enjoy more than hers.

The joys of marriage will be far greater because of the character and love of our bridegroom. I rejoice for Nanci and for me that we'll both be married to the most wonderful person in the universe. He's already the one we love most—there is no competition. On earth, the closer we draw to Him, the closer we draw to each other. Surely the same will be true in Heaven. What an honor it'll be to always know that God chose us for each other on this old earth so that we might have a foretaste of life with Him on the New Earth.

I hope you underlined phrases like *best friend, closest sister,* and *love most.* How will those phrases apply to Christ and you as part of His bride in Heaven? _____

_____

_____

How can the phrases still have meaning for you and family members? _____

_____

_____

Jesus said the institution of human marriage would end, having fulfilled its purpose. But He never hinted that deep relationships between married people would end.

What about our children? What about my daughters and sons-in-law and closest friends? There's every reason to believe we'll pick right up in Heaven with relationships from earth. We'll gain many new ones but will continue to deepen the old ones. I think we'll especially enjoy connecting with those we faced tough times with on earth and saying, "Did you ever imagine Heaven would be so wonderful?"

What have you considered today that makes you love Christ more or anticipate being with Him in Heaven?

_____

_____

_____

_____

DAY 5

What Will We Experience Together?

Jesus told us we'll dine with Abraham, Isaac, and Jacob (see Matt. 8:11). Dinner is not only about good food and drink but also a time for building relationships, talking together, and telling stories.

I'd like to ask Mary to tell stories about Jesus as a child. I'd enjoy talking with Simeon, Anna, Elizabeth, and John the Baptist. I'm eager to listen to Moses tell about his times with God on the mountain. I'd like to ask Elijah about being taken away in the chariot and Enoch (and Enoch's wife) about his being caught up by God. I want to talk with Mary, Martha, and their brother Lazarus. I'll ask people to fill in the blanks of the great stories in Scripture and church history. I want to hear a few million new stories. One at a time, of course, and spread out over thousands of years. I imagine we'll relish these great stories, ask questions, laugh together, and shake our heads in amazement.

What stories (from Scripture or family) would you like to hear?

_____

_____

We'll each have our own stories to tell also—and the memories and skills to tell them well. Right now, today, we are living the lives from which such stories will be drawn. We'll have new adventures on the New Earth, but I suspect the old stories from this life will always interest us.

What story would you like to tell?

_____

_____

I look forward to reconnecting with many old friends as well as my mom and dad. I look forward to thanking C. S. Lewis, Francis Schaeffer, and A. W. Tozer for how their writings changed me. I anticipate meeting William Carey, Hudson and Maria Taylor, Amy Carmichael, Jim Elliot, Charles Spurgeon, Dwight L. Moody, Harriet Beecher Stowe, some of the Amistad slaves, and a host of others.

Who's on your list?

_____

_____

How are you serving Christ today so that you may be on someone else's list? _____

_____

IF OUR LOVED ONES ARE IN HELL, WON'T THAT SPOIL HEAVEN?

Some people argue that people in Heaven won't know hell exists because it would spoil our joy. But this would make Heaven's joy dependent on ignorance, which is nowhere taught in Scripture.

How could we enjoy Heaven knowing that a loved one is in hell? J. I. Packer offers an answer that's difficult but biblical: "God will judge justly, and all angels, saints, and martyrs will praise him for it. So it seems inescapable that we shall, with them, approve the judgment of persons—rebels—whom we have known and loved.[8]

In Heaven, we will see with a new and far better perspective. We'll fully concur with God's judgment on the wicked. The martyrs in Heaven call on God to judge evil people on earth (see Rev. 6:9-11).

Read Revelation 18:20. How do the people in Heaven respond?

_____

_____

We'll never question God's justice, wondering how He could send good people to hell. Rather, we'll be overwhelmed with His grace, marveling at what He did to send bad people to Heaven. We will no longer have any illusion that fallen people are good without Christ. We'll see

"Rejoice over her, heaven, and you saints, apostles, and prophets, because God has executed your judgment on her."

REVELATION 18:20

clearly that God revealed Himself to each person and gave opportunity for each to seek and respond to Him (see Rom. 1:18—2:16). Every unbeliever has rejected God and His self-revelation in creation, conscience, or the gospel. Everyone deserves hell. No one deserves Heaven. Jesus went to the cross to offer salvation to "the whole world" (1 John 2:2).

We'll embrace God's holiness and justice. We'll praise Him for His goodness and grace. God will be our source of joy. Hell's small and distant shadow will not interfere with God's greatness or our joy in Him. All of this should motivate us to share the gospel of Christ with family, friends, neighbors, and the whole world.

Although it will inevitably sound harsh, I offer this further thought: In a sense, none of our loved ones will be in hell—only some whom we once loved. Our love for our companions in Heaven will be directly linked to God, the central object of our love. We will see Him in them. We will not love those in hell because when we see Jesus as He is, we will love only—and will only want to love—whoever and whatever pleases and glorifies and reflects Him. What we loved in those who died without Christ was God's beauty we once saw in them. When God forever withdraws from them, I think they'll no longer bear His image and no longer reflect His beauty. Although they will be the same people, without God they'll be stripped of all the qualities we loved. Therefore, paradoxically, in a sense they will not be the people we loved.

I cannot prove biblically what I've just stated, but I think it rings true, even if the thought is horrifying. We may be certain: Hell will have no power over Heaven; hell's misery will never veto Heaven's joy.

> Hell's small and distant shadow will not interfere with God's greatness or our joy in Him.

WILL WE SHARE DISCOVERIES TOGETHER?

Friendships emerge from shared experiences. Doing things together bonds us. The same will be true on the New Earth. We'll be knit together as we discover together the wonders of God and his universe.

Describe a time when you uniquely bonded with a group because of an experience you shared. _____

_____

_____

How do you feel about those people?

_____

_____

_____

Suppose you're taking an extended family vacation, but you arrive at the vacation destination four days after most of your family members. They describe all the sights you've missed. What's your reaction? You're happy the family's been having a good time, but you feel left out. You've missed the bonding that came with the common experience.

Wouldn't it be great to travel to Heaven together, simultaneously? Wouldn't it be great to be like Lewis and Clark, discovering together the wonders of the new world? In fact, that's precisely what Scripture tells us will happen. Though we go to the present Heaven one at a time as we die, all of us will be charter citizens of the New Earth. We'll be resurrected together and set foot on the New Earth together.

We'll share our discoveries together, grabbing each other by the hand and saying, "You can't believe what Jesus made—an animal I've never dreamed of. You've got to come see it!"

Unlike the hypothetical experience of arriving late to your vacation destination, you won't have missed out on the beginning of the New Earth. You will be there first—with everyone else. When someone asks, "Remember when God made the New Earth and brought the New Jerusalem down out of Heaven and came to dwell among us in the new world He built for us?" all of us will nod our heads and say, "Sure, I remember—how could I ever forget? I was there!"

What will it be like for those who died weak and elderly to take their first steps in their resurrected bodies? In Lewis's _The Last Battle_, on entering Heaven, Lord Digory says he and Lady Polly have been "unstiffened."[9] He adds, "We stopped feeling old." I look forward to seeing my mother and father "unstiffened" again—and to being completely unstiffened myself!

How glorious it will be for grandchildren and grandparents—and great-grandchildren and grandparents who never knew each other before—to enjoy youth together in the cities, fields, hillsides, and waters of the New Earth. To walk together, discover together, be amazed together—and praise Jesus together. Forever.

WILL WE REGAIN LOST RELATIONAL OPPORTUNITIES?

In Heaven we'll have unlimited time. I'm eager to spend time again with my childhood friend Jerry, who died years ago. I anticipate meeting him in Heaven and picking up right where we left off.

Do you have family and friends you wish you could spend more time with? ❏ yes ❏ no

With whom would you most like to spend more time?

_____

_____

What would you enjoy doing together?

_____

_____

_____

A young woman was visiting a missionary in Eastern Europe and asked her, "Isn't it hard being so far away from your grown children and missing important events in their lives?"

"Sure," the missionary replied. "But in Heaven we'll have all the time together we want. Right now there's kingdom work that needs to be done." This woman knows where her true home is—and that life there will be real life and that relationships among God's people will resume in ways even better than what we've known here. We may not be able to regain opportunities we passed up due to unfaithfulness, but I believe we'll regain whatever we passed up in order to faithfully serve God.

How could Jesus' words in Luke 6:21-23 confirm the statements above? _____

_____

Consider the millions of Christians who suffered and died in prison because of their faith, who were snatched from their families, deprived of opportunities they craved. Wouldn't it be just like Jesus to reward them on the New Earth with opportunities to do the very things they missed—and far better things as well?

Heaven offers more than comfort; it offers compensation. In the same way that the hungry will fill up in Heaven and those who weep will laugh, will those who suffer tragedy experience a compensating victory? Maybe all my mom missed because she died before our daughters became adults will be hers in Heaven. Maybe those who lost infants to miscarriage and disease and accidents will be given makeup time with them in the new world.

If a father dies before his daughter's wedding and if they are Christians, then he'll be there for her ultimate wedding—to Christ. If he never lived to see his believing son play basketball, he'll not only see him play on earth but also play with him on the New Earth. And his children will enjoy the pleasure of seeing the look of utter approval on their father's face ... and their Father's face.

Write a note to Jesus expressing your thoughts and feelings about this week's study. _____

_____

_____

_____

_____

1. Arthur E. Travis, *Where on Earth Is Heaven?* (Nashville: Broadman, 1974), 24.
2. Ibid., 30.
3. James M. Campbell, *Heaven Opened* (New York: Revell, 1924), 169.
4. Randy Alcorn, *Deadline* (Sisters, OR: Multnomah, 1994), 238.
5. John Calvin, quoted in Colleen McDannell and Bernhard Lang, *Heaven: A History* (New York: Vintage Books, 1988), 155.
6. Richard Baxter, *The Practical Works of Richard Baxter* (Grand Rapids: Baker, 1981), 97.
7. George MacDonald, quoted in Herbert Lockyer, *Death and the Life Hereafter* (Grand Rapids: Baker, 1975), 65.
8. J. I. Packer, "Hell's Final Enigma," *Christianity Today* (April 22, 2002): 84.
9. C. S. Lewis, *The Last Battle* (New York: Collier, 1956), 139.

What Will We Do in Heaven?

DAY 1

What Will We Know and Learn?

We commonly hear people say things such as, "We don't understand now, but in Heaven we'll know everything."

To say that we'll know everything when we're in Heaven is misleading. God alone is omniscient. When we die, we'll see things far more clearly, and we'll know much more than we do now, but we'll never know everything.

The Apostle Paul wrote: "Now we see but a poor reflection as in a mirror; then we shall see face to face. Now I know in part; then I shall know fully, even as I am fully known" (1 Cor. 13:12).

Read the context verses surrounding 1 Corinthians 13:12. According to verse 8, what was Paul talking about?

❑ ways of obtaining general knowledge about everything

❑ ways of knowing God and His will

In *Systematic Theology* Wayne Grudem says, "First Corinthians 13:12 does not say that we will be omniscient or know everything (Paul could have said we will know all things ... if he had wished to do so), but, rightly translated, it simply says that we will know in a fuller or more intensive way ... without any error or misconceptions in our knowledge."[1]

In Heaven we'll be flawless, but not knowing everything isn't a flaw. It's part of being finite. Righteous angels don't know everything, and they long to know more (see 1 Pet. 1:12). They're flawless but finite. We should expect to long for greater knowledge, as angels do. And we'll spend eternity gaining the greater knowledge we'll seek.

"Angels desire to look into these things."

1 PETER 1:12, HCSB

WILL WE REALLY LEARN?

In a Gallup poll of people's perspectives about Heaven, only 18 percent thought people would grow intellectually in Heaven.[2]

Read Ephesians 2:6-7. In what activity did Paul tell us God will be involved during the coming ages?

❑ seating us in Heaven

❑ showing the riches of His grace

❑ building scale models of extinct species

Those who know Jesus as Savior are already seated with Him in Heaven. The word *show* means "to reveal." The phrase *in the coming ages* clearly indicates this will be a progressive, ongoing revelation in which we learn more and more about God's grace.

I frequently learn new things about my wife, daughters, and closest friends, even though I've known them for many years. If I can always be learning something new about finite, limited human beings, surely I'll learn infinitely more about Jesus. None of us will ever begin to exhaust His depths.

"God raised us up with Christ and seated us with him in the heavenly realms in Christ Jesus, in order that in the coming ages he might show the incomparable riches of his grace, expressed in his kindness to us in Christ Jesus."

EPHESIANS 2:6-7

Jesus said to His disciples, "Learn from me" (Matt. 11:29). On the New Earth we'll have the privilege of sitting at Jesus' feet as Mary did, walking with Him over the countryside as His disciples did, always learning from Him. In Heaven we'll continually learn new things about God, going ever deeper in our understanding.

It was God—not Satan—who made us learners. God doesn't want us to stop learning. What He wants to stop is the obstacles that prevent us from learning.

What genuine obstacles now prevent you from actively seeking all the new knowledge and better understanding you'd like?

_____

_____

_____

Many see the process of learning as a negative, but don't you love to discover something new—especially about a subject of personal interest? On the New Earth, some of our greatest discoveries may relate to the lives we're living right now. Columnist and commentator Paul Harvey made a career of telling *The Rest of the Story*. That's exactly what we'll discover in Heaven again and again—the rest of the story. We'll be stunned to learn how God orchestrated the events of our lives to influence people we may have forgotten about.

About what events in your life do you particularly long to hear "the rest of the story"?

_____

_____

_____

_____

Occasionally we hear stories that provide us a small taste of what we'll learn in eternity. One morning after I spoke at a church, a young woman came up to me and asked, "Do you remember a young man sitting next to you on a plane headed to college? You gave him your novel *Dead-*

line." I give away a lot of my books on planes, but after some prompting, I remembered him. He was an unbeliever. We talked about Jesus, and I gave him the book and prayed for him as we got off the plane.

I was amazed when the young woman said to me, "He told me he never contacted you, so you wouldn't know what happened. He got to college, checked into the dorm, sat down, and read your book. When he was done, he confessed his sins and gave his life to Jesus. And I can honestly tell you, he's the most dynamic Christian I've ever met."

All I did was talk a little, give him a book, and pray for him. But if the young woman hadn't told me, I wouldn't have had a clue what had happened. That story reminded me how many great stories await us in Heaven and how many we may not hear until we've been there a long time. We won't ever know everything, and even what we will know, we won't know all at once. We'll be learners, forever. Few things excite me more than that.

WHAT WILL IT BE LIKE TO LEARN?

Could God impart knowledge so we immediately know things when we get to Heaven? Certainly. Adam and Eve didn't go to school. They were created, it appears, with an initial vocabulary. But Adam and Eve are the exceptions. Every other person has learned by experience and study. And Adam and Eve were learners the rest of their lives.

When we enter Heaven, we'll presumably begin with the knowledge we had at the time of our death. God may enhance our knowledge and will correct countless wrong perceptions. I imagine He'll reveal many new things to us, then set us on a course of continual learning, paralleling Adam and Eve's. Once we're in resurrection bodies with resurrected brains, our capacity to learn may increase. Perhaps angel guardians or loved ones already in Heaven will be assigned to tutor and orient us.

We will also study. Martin Luther is reported to have said, "If God had all the answers in his right hand, and the struggle to reach those answers in his left, I would choose God's left hand." Why? Because it's not only truth we want, it's also the pleasure of *learning* the truth. God reveals himself to us in the process of our learning, often in bite-sized chunks, fit for our finite minds.

Describe a time when you have felt particular satisfaction because you learned something.

_____

_____

_____

God's truth will be living and vital, never dry and dusty. We will dialogue about truth not to impress each other but to enrich each other and ourselves as we discover more and more about God.

To study creation is to study the Creator. Science should be worshipful discovery because the heavens and all creation declare God's glory. God reveals his character in flowers, waterfalls, animals, and planets. God's name is written large in nature, in His beauty, organization, skill, precision, and attention to detail. He's the Master Artist. On the New Earth everything will be a lens through which we see him. Biology, zoology, chemistry, astronomy, physics—all will be the study of God.

So much remains to discover in this universe, but we have so little time and opportunity to do it. The list of books I haven't read, music I've never heard, and places I haven't been is unending. There's much more to know. I look forward to discovering new things in Heaven—forever. At the end of each day I'll have the same amount of time left as I did the day before. The things I didn't learn that day, the people I didn't see, the things I couldn't do—I can still learn, see, or do the next day. Places won't crumble, people won't die, and neither will I.

In Heaven we'll contemplate God's person and works, talking long over dinner and tea, on walks and in living rooms, by rivers and fires. Intellectual curiosity isn't part of the curse—it is God's blessing on His image-bearers. He made us with fertile, curious minds so that we might seek truth and find him, our greatest source of pleasure. In Heaven our intellectual curiosity will surely surface—and be satisfied—only to surface and be satisfied again and again.

DAY 2

Will Work Be Engaging?
Will We Express Creativity?

"Jubal ... was the father of all who play the lyre and the flute. ... Tubal-cain ... made all kinds of bronze and iron tools."

GENESIS 4:21,22, HCSB

The New Earth includes a carryover of culture and nations. History won't start over with the New Earth, anymore than history started over when Adam and Eve were banished from the garden.

Culture won't regress to Eden, where musical instruments hadn't yet been invented or where metalworking and countless other skills hadn't yet been developed (Gen. 4:20-22). The fact that God mentioned in Scripture these and other examples of technological progress suggests that He approved of people's using their creativity and skills to develop society, even though they were hampered by the curse.

Some expect the New Earth to be a return to Eden, with no technology or the accomplishments of civilization. But that doesn't fit the biblical picture of the great city, the New Jerusalem. Nor is it logical. Would we expect on the New Earth a literal reinvention of the wheel?

Consider this analogy: A teenager has been sick from infancy and is suddenly healed. Does he become a baby again? No. He's a well teenager. He doesn't go back and start over from the point his health went bad. Rather, he continues from where he is, going on from there. He doesn't abandon the knowledge and skills he's developed. He's simply far more capable of using them, now that he's been healed.

WILL OUR WORK BE ENGAGING?

On the New Earth, God will give us renewed minds and marvelously constructed bodies. We'll be whole people, full of energy and vision. James Campbell said, "The work on the other side, whatever be its character, will be adapted to each one's special aptitude and powers. It will be the work he can do best; the work that will give the fullest play to all that is within him."[3]

Even under the curse we catch glimpses of how work can be enriching, how it can build relationships, and how it can help us to improve. Work stretches and fulfills us. The God who created us to do good works (Eph. 2:10) will not cancel this purpose when He resurrects us. The Bible's picture of resurrected people at work in a vibrant society on a resurrected Earth couldn't be more compelling: We're going to help God run the universe (Luke 19:11-27).

We will serve God in Heaven. Work in Heaven won't be frustrating or fruitless; instead, it will involve lasting accomplishment, unhindered by decay and fatigue, enhanced by unlimited resources. We'll approach our work with the enthusiasm we bring to our favorite sport or hobby.

In Heaven, we'll reign with Christ, exercise leadership and authority, and make important decisions. We'll set goals, devise plans, and share ideas. Our best work days on the present Earth—those days when everything turns out better than we planned, when we get everything done on time, and when everyone on the team pulls together and enjoys each other—are just a small foretaste of the joy our work will bring us on the New Earth.

What type of work do you find most satisfying?

_____

_____

_____

How might that work be enhanced on the New Earth?

_____

_____

_____

HOW WILL WE EXPRESS OUR CREATIVITY?

In this world, even under the curse, human imagination and skill has produced some remarkable works. The statues of Easter Island. Stonehenge. Shakespeare's plays. Beethoven's Ninth Symphony. Baseball. Heart transplants. Prenatal surgery. Microwave ovens. The space shuttle. Chocolate ice cream. Pecan pie. Sports cars. It's a list that never ends.

> *"For we are His creation—created in Christ Jesus for good works, which God prepared ahead of time so that we should walk in them."*
>
> EPHESIANS 2:10, HCSB

With the resources God will lavishly give us on the New Earth, what will we be able to accomplish together? When we think about this, we should be like children anticipating Christmas—sneaking out of bed to see what's under the Christmas tree.

I imagine that people will express creativity in designing clothes. The precious stones of the New Jerusalem suggest jewelry may have a place on the New Earth. Some people wear jewelry now for status, but on the New Earth, God-made jewels worn by people made in the image of God will reflect the Creator's beauty.

What does Isaiah 65:21 specifically tell us we'll do on the New Earth?

_____

_____

No doubt we'll decorate buildings on the scale of the New Jerusalem. Human builders will learn from God's design, just as Leonardo da Vinci learned by studying birds while working on his flying machine. What will clear-thinking human beings—unhindered by sin and the barriers that separate us—be able to design and build? What would Galileo, Leonardo, Edison, or Einstein achieve if they could live even a thousand years unhindered by the curse? What will we achieve when we have resurrected bodies with resurrected minds, working together forever?

DOES GOD VALUE CRAFTSMANSHIP?

The first person Scripture describes as "filled with the Spirit" wasn't a prophet or priest. He was a craftsman. God gifted and called Bezalel to be a skilled laborer, a master craftsman, a God-glorifying artist (Ex. 31–36). Bezalel and Oholiab were not only to create works of art but also to train apprentices to do so. God gave both the gifting and calling.

If you don't believe craftsmanship will be an important part of the New Earth, read Exodus 25–40. God told His people in exquisite detail how to sew clothing, what colors to use, how to construct the furniture for the ark of the covenant and tabernacle, what stones to put on the high priest's breastplate, and so on.

"I have filled him with the Spirit of God, with skill, ability and knowledge in all kinds of crafts." EXODUS 31:3

Those who imagine that spirituality is something ethereal and invisible—unrelated to our physical skills, craftsmanship, and cultural development—fail to understand Scripture. God's instructions and His delight in the gifts He imparts to people to accomplish these tasks makes clear what we should expect in Heaven: greater works of craftsmanship and construction, unhindered by sin and death.

WILL THERE BE TECHNOLOGY AND MACHINERY?

Technology is a God-given aspect of human capability that enables us to fulfill His command to exercise dominion. We will find harps, trumpets, and other man-made objects in the present Heaven. What should we expect to find on the New Earth? Tables, chairs, cabinets, wagons, machinery, transportation, sports equipment, and much more. It's a narrow view of both God and mankind to imagine that God can be pleased and glorified with a trumpet but not a desk, computer, or baseball bat. Will there be new inventions? Refinements of old inventions? Why not? We'll live in resurrected bodies on a resurrected earth. The God who gave people creativity surely won't take it back, will He?

What does Romans 11:29 tell us about God's gifts and calling?

When God gave Eden to Adam and Eve, He expected them to develop it. He'll give us the New Earth and expect the same of us. But this time we'll succeed! This time no human accomplishment, no cultural masterpiece, no technological achievement will be marred by sin and death. All will fully serve God's purposes and bring Him glory.

Something in the human constitution loves to create, experiment, and play with machinery. This isn't a modern development; it's inherent in exercising dominion over creation.

If mankind had never sinned, would we have invented the wheel and created machinery? Certainly. On the New Earth, shouldn't we expect machinery made for the good of mankind and the glory of God? On the New Earth people might invent machinery that could take us to the far ends of the New Milky Way, to other galaxies and beyond. Why not? Is this notion more unthinkable than it once was to imagine sailing a ship across an ocean, flying a plane across the world, or landing a spacecraft on the moon? Because people in this fallen world have extended their dominion beyond our current earth, might we not expect people on the New Earth to extend their Christ-exalting reach into the new universe?

God will provide for us a renewed natural universe and a new city with the best of human culture from the old earth. But where civilization goes from there will be up to us. For just as God called Adam and Eve, God calls us to develop a Christ-pleasing culture and to rule the world to His glory.

What have you considered today that most excites you about living in the New Heavens and the New Earth?

_____

_____

_____

_____

What would you like to tell the Father who has created such an amazing future for us?

_____

_____

_____

_____

_____

_____

God is a Creator, and He created us to be creators. Hence, what we create is an extension of God's creation. He accepts, embraces, and delights in our creation—even as He did the names that Adam gave the animals. He delights in us just as we delight in our own children's creativity.

DAY 3

Will There Be Arts, Entertainment, and Sports?

Music, dancing, storytelling, art, entertainment, drama, and sports have played major roles in human culture. Will they remain a part of our lives on the New Earth? I'm convinced the answer is yes.

WHAT ROLE WILL MUSIC PLAY IN HEAVEN?

The 144,000 redeemed from the earth will sing a "new song" before God's throne (Rev. 14:2-3). People in Paradise will sing the "song of Moses"— likely the song of Exodus 15, rejoicing in the redemption of Passover (Rev. 15:2-3). We'll sing both old and new songs, songs written on earth and songs written in Heaven.

On earth, creative, artistic, and skilled people sing and play instruments to glorify God. The Apostle John spoke of trumpets and harps in the present Heaven (8:7-13; 15:2). If we'll have musical instruments in our preresurrected state, how much more should we expect to find them on the New Earth?

"I will sing to the LORD all my life; I will sing praise to my God as long as I live." PSALM 104:33

What is your relationship to music on this present earth? Check any that apply.
- ❏ I can't imagine life without the joy of music.
- ❏ I can hardly play the radio without an extra helping of static.
- ❏ I long to play a musical instrument well.
- ❏ Playing music is one of the great joys of my life.
- ❏ Other _____

Music is transcendent. That's why people devote so much of themselves to it and gain such pleasure in it. In Heaven God will unleash our creativity, not confine it. As a musical novice, I might compose something worthy of Bach. What kind of music do you suppose he will compose?

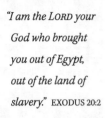

"I am the LORD your God who brought you out of Egypt, out of the land of slavery." EXODUS 20:2

WILL WE TELL STORIES?

God regularly reminds His people of His past faithfulness (Ex. 20:2). History, when viewed accurately, teaches us about God and about ourselves. It's the record of our failure to rule the earth righteously, the record of God's sovereign and gracious redemption.

The angels will be able to recount the creation of the original universe (Job 38:1-7). But we'll have an even greater story to tell—the creation of the new universe (Rev. 21:1-4).

When we gather at meals and other times, we'll tell stories of past battles. We'll recite God's acts of grace in our lives. (Are we practicing this now?) Some of those acts of grace we didn't understand at the time; some we resented. But we'll see then with an eternal perspective.

Just as we're now captivated by a person's story of heroism or rescue from danger, we'll be enthralled by the stories in Heaven. I can't wait to hear John Newton's story and William Wilberforce's and Mary Magdalene's. Wouldn't you love to hear from the angel who strengthened Christ in Gethsemane (see Luke 22:43)? Imagine sitting around campfires on the New Earth, wide-eyed at the adventures recounted.

WILL WE REALLY LAUGH?

"If you're not allowed to laugh in heaven, I don't want to go there."[4] Mark Twain didn't say that. It was Martin Luther. Am I just speculating about laughter? No. I can point to Scripture passages worth memorizing.

What does Luke 6:21 promise in our future?

_____

_____

Write Luke 6:21 on a card and begin memorizing the verse. Don't forget to praise Jesus for His promise!

When will we be satisfied? In Heaven. When will we laugh? In Heaven. Can we be certain of that? Yes. Jesus tells us precisely when this promise will be fulfilled: "Rejoice in that day and leap for joy, because great is your reward in heaven" (Luke 6:23).

Just as Jesus promised satisfaction as a reward in Heaven, He also promised laughter. Take any group of rejoicing people, and what do you hear? Laughter. It is God's gift to humanity, a gift that will only be raised to new levels after our resurrection.

The reward of those who mourn now will be laughter later. Passages such as Luke 6 gave the early Christians strength to endure persecution. Only followers of Christ can laugh in the face of persecution and death because they know that their present trouble isn't all there is. They know that someday they will laugh.

The fact that we could wonder whether there's laughter in Heaven shows how skewed our perspective is. C. S. Lewis said, "Joy is the serious business of Heaven."[5]

One of Satan's great lies is that God—and good—is joyless and humorless, while Satan—and evil—brings pleasure and satisfaction. In fact, Satan is humorless. Sin didn't bring him joy; it forever stripped him of it. In contrast, who is the most intelligent, creative, witty, and joyful human being in the universe? Jesus Christ. Whose laughter will be loudest and most contagious on the New Earth? Jesus Christ's.

How do you think it would change our attitude if every day we reflected on the great joy of our Lord (Neh. 8:10)?

When we face difficulty and discouragement in this world, we must keep our eyes on the source of our joy. Remember, "Blessed are you who weep now, for you will laugh" (Luke 6:21).

WILL THERE BE SPORTS?

Just as we can look forward to cultural endeavors such as art, drama, and music on the New Earth, we can assume that we'll also enjoy sports there. Sports and our enjoyment of them aren't a result of the fall. I have no doubt that sinless people would have invented athletics, with probably more variations than we have today. Sports suit our minds and our bodies. They're an expression of our God-designed humanity.

"Nehemiah said, 'Go and enjoy choice food and sweet drinks, and send some to those who have nothing prepared. This day is sacred to our Lord. Do not grieve, for the joy of the LORD is your strength.'"

NEHEMIAH 8:10

What kinds of new sports and activities might we engage in on the New Earth? The possibilities are limitless. Perhaps we'll participate in sports that were once too risky. And just as we might have stimulating conversations with theologians and writers in Heaven, we might also have the opportunity to play our favorite sports with some of our favorite sports heroes. How would you like to play golf with Payne Stewart or shoot hoops with David Robinson? How would you like to play catch with Andy Pettitte or go for a run with Jesse Owens or Eric Liddell?

How do you react to the idea of sports in Heaven?

_____

_____

People have told me, "But there can't be athletics in Heaven because competition brings out the worst in people." It's true that some people's sin spills over during athletic competition. But in Heaven, there will be no worst in us to bring out. People further object: "But in sports, someone has to lose. And in Heaven no one could lose." Who says so? I've thoroughly enjoyed many tennis matches and 10-kilometer races that I've lost. Losing a game isn't evil. It's not part of the curse. To say that "everyone would have to win in Heaven" underestimates the nature of resurrected humanity.

CAN THERE BE THRILLS WITHOUT RISK?

A sincere young man told me that no matter what I might say, Heaven _must_ be boring. Why? "Because you can't appreciate good without bad, light without darkness, or safety without danger. If Heaven is safe, if there's no risk, it has to be boring."

His first mistake was assuming there's no good without bad. God said earth was "very good" before there was sin or anything bad (Gen. 1:31). Adam and Eve enjoyed Eden's goodness before experiencing sin's evil. This young man's next mistake was believing that a person has to currently see evil at work to appreciate good and to currently be in danger to appreciate safety.

My father lived through the Great Depression. He told me stories of sleeping outside in the cold, covered only with newspaper. Dad first told me these stories 50 years after the fact. He'd been able to sleep inside for half a century, but he vividly remembered the hard times. Suppose someone had said to him, "You can't appreciate having a warm fire and a warm bed unless there's the threat of sleeping out in the cold tonight." He'd say, "You think I'll ever forget those days?" His memories didn't make him miserable; they made him grateful.

After our bodily resurrection, we'll still remember the darkness and dangers of this life. We'll contrast our past experiences with the light and safety of the New Earth, and we'll be profoundly grateful.

The young man went on to say, "I like extreme sports. I enjoy working hard and sweating. But there won't be any challenges in Heaven. If there's no risk of falling and dying, it can't be really fun."

How would you respond to the young man's reasoning?

_____

_____

Where does Scripture say there won't be challenges or hard work in Heaven? Were there no challenges in Eden? The Bible says there will be no more evil or suffering—not that there won't be challenges.

Did Adam and Eve work hard? Did they sweat and get sore? Everyone who enjoys sports knows that there's a "good tired" and a "good sore." It's satisfying. It's part of knowing you've stretched yourself. Why wouldn't our resurrection bodies sweat? God didn't create sweat glands after the fall, did He?

Why couldn't we tumble while climbing on the New Earth? Won't there be gravity? Adam and Eve couldn't die, but couldn't they skin their knees? Did God originally create bodies without nerve endings? Perhaps they could fall, do minor damage, and then heal quickly. We're told that on the New Earth there'll be no more death, crying, or pain (Rev. 21:4). But we're also told, "The leaves of the tree are for the healing of the nations" (22:2). No one will suffer or die on the New Earth, but this passage suggests enough injury to require healing.

But even if there's absolutely no injury, fear of injury and death aren't essential to excitement, are they? If you knew that in 30 years there hadn't been a single fatality on a roller coaster, couldn't you still be thrilled by the ride? When our daughters were small, they experienced the thrill of rides at the fair as I held them tightly. The fun was in moving fast, spinning around, feeling the wind on their faces. In the same way, couldn't we parachute from a plane and have an exhilarating free fall even if we knew there was a zero percent chance of dying? (Some of us might consider that more fun, not less.)

I believe our resurrection bodies will have adrenaline and the ability to feel. On the New Earth we may experience adventures that make our current mountain climbs, surfing, skydiving, and upside-down roller coaster rides seem tame. Why do I say this? It's more than wishful thinking. It's an argument from design. We take pleasure in exhilarating experiences not because of sin but because God wired us this way. We weren't made to sit all day in dark rooms, watching actors pretend to live and athletes do what we can't. We were made to live vibrant lives. Because God's design wasn't an accident—because He doesn't make mistakes—we can be sure that excitement and exhilaration will be more, not less, a part of our experience in Heaven than it is now.

I told you I wanted to challenge your concept of Heaven. So how am I doing? What ideas have you rethought this week?

_____

_____

_____

What difference does it make?

_____

_____

Skydiving without a parachute? Maybe, maybe not. Scuba diving without an air tank? I hope so. Those who know God and believe his promise of bodily resurrection can dream great dreams.

One day we will live those dreams.

DAY 4

Will Our Dreams Be Fulfilled and Missed Opportunities Regained?

Are you living with the disappointment of unfulfilled dreams? In Heaven you'll find their fulfillment! Did poverty, poor health, war, or lack of time prevent you from pursuing a dream? Did you never get to finish building that boat or painting that picture or writing that book—or reading that pile of books? Good news. On the New Earth you will have a second chance to do what you dreamed of doing—and far more besides.

Name three dreams you look forward to fulfilling in Heaven.

_____

_____

_____

Which is most important to you and why?

_____

_____

We don't want to live as some other kind of creatures in some other world. We want to be sinless, healthy people living on an earth without conflict, disease, disappointment, and death. We want to be the people who live in the kind of world where the deepest longings of our hearts really do come true. That is exactly what God's Word promises us.

Our failure to grasp this hurts us in countless ways. We become discouraged, supposing that if we're handicapped, we'll never know the joy of running in a meadow or the pleasure of swimming. Or if we weren't married—or didn't have a good marriage—we'll never know the joy of marriage.

What negative effects on people have you seen because of these kinds of disappointments?

❑ blaming God for injustice

❑ discouragement and depression

❑ poor choices seeking immediate pleasures

❑ other _____

We speak of the apparent injustices in the world as the problem of evil. Many people reject Christ because they don't believe God is fair.

How does it change your perception of the problem of evil when you consider God's future fulfillments that await His children?

_____

_____

_____

On the New Earth, in perfect bodies, we'll run through meadows and swim in lakes. We'll have the most exciting and fulfilling marriage there's ever been, a marriage so glorious and complete there will be no purpose for another. Jesus Himself will be our bridegroom!

The smartest person God ever created in this world may never have learned to read because he or she had no opportunity. The most musically gifted person may never have touched a musical instrument. The greatest athlete may never have competed in a game. The sport you're best at may be a sport you've never tried, your favorite hobby one you've never thought of. Living under the curse means we miss many opportunities. The reversing of the curse in the final resurrection means we'll regain opportunities and inherit many more besides.

ARE WE PAST OUR PEAKS?

I write this book well aware that I won't be on earth much longer. Oh, I might last another 30 years. But it could be 20, 10, 5, or 1—1 year, day, or hour. By the time this study is published, I could be a true expert on the present Heaven—as a resident. By the time you read it, I may have died years ago. Our time here is short. But when we consider "here" is under the curse and "there" is freedom from that curse, then why would people in their right minds want to be here instead of there?

When Nanci's father was dying, he was falling further and further from his peak. I heard her say to someone on the phone, "Life is closing in on him, but he's headed the right direction." It's paradoxical, isn't it? But true. The further we drop from our earthly peak, the closer we get to the present Heaven and ultimately to the New Earth. For the Christian, death is the doorway to the Christ who has defeated death and will swallow it up. Therefore, to be headed toward death is to be headed in the right direction.

Understanding that our peak doesn't come in this life should radically change our view of deteriorating health, which otherwise would produce discouragement, regret, anger, envy, and resentment. Elderly people could envy and resent the young for what they can do. People handicapped from birth could envy and resent others for what they can do. But when the elderly and handicapped recognize that their experiences on the New Earth will be far better than the best anyone else is experiencing here and now, it brings anticipation, contentment, consolation, and the ability to fully rejoice in the activities of the young and healthy, without envy or regret.

People without Christ can only look back to when they were at their best, never to regain it. Memories are all they have, and even those memories fade. But elderly or bedridden Christians don't look back to the peak of their prowess. They look forward to it.

When we Christians sit in wheelchairs or lie in beds or feel our bodies shutting down, let's remind ourselves, "I haven't passed my peak. I haven't yet come close to it. The strongest and healthiest I've ever felt is a faint hint of what I'll be in my resurrected body on the New Earth."

The time may come when I won't be able to play tennis, ride bikes, drive, write books, or read them. I may suffer terribly before I die. Someday my wife or my daughters may sit beside my bed, lovingly assuring me that I've been imagining things again. I don't look forward to that. But I do look beyond it. I look first to being with my Jesus, second to being with loved ones, third to the bodily resurrection, and fourth to

> For Christians, death is the doorway to Christ.

setting foot on my eternal home—the New Earth. It makes me want to shout and cry and laugh just thinking about it.

I don't look back nostalgically at wonderful moments in my life, wistfully thinking the best days are behind me. I look at them as fore-tastes of an eternity of better things. Everything done in dependence on God will bear fruit for eternity. This life need not be wasted. In small and often unnoticed acts of service to Christ, we can invest this life in eternity, where today's faithfulness will forever pay rich dividends.

As we draw to the end, what difference will it really make to live sacrificial lives on earth now?

_____

_____

_____

_____

"Thanks, Lord, that the best is yet to be." That's my prayer. God will one day clear away sin, death, and sorrow, as surely as builders clear away debris so they can begin new construction.

DAY 5

Are You Living in Light of Heaven?

Imagine someone takes you to a party. You see a few friends there, enjoy a couple of good conversations, a little laughter, and some decent appe-tizers. The party's all right, but you keep hoping it will get better. Give it another hour, and maybe it will. Suddenly your friend says, "I need to take you home."

Now?

The buds of this life's greatest moments don't shrivel and die; they blossom into greater moments, each to be treasured, none to be lost.

You're disappointed—nobody wants to leave a party early—but you leave, and your friend drops you off at your house. As you approach the door, you're feeling all alone and sorry for yourself. As you open the door and reach for the light switch, you sense someone's there. Your heart's in your throat. You flip on the light.

"Surprise!" Your house is full of smiling people, familiar faces.

It's a party—for you. You smell your favorites—barbecued ribs and pecan pie right out of the oven. The tables are full. It's a feast. You recognize the guests, people you haven't seen for a long time. Then, one by one, the people you most enjoyed at the other party show up at your house, grinning. This turns out to be the real party. You realize that if you'd stayed longer at the other party, as you'd wanted, you wouldn't be at the real party—you'd be away from it.

If this party illustration were a parable about Heaven, how would you explain it? _____

_____

_____

Christians faced with terminal illness or imminent death often feel they're leaving the party before it's over. They have to go home early. They're disappointed, thinking of all they'll miss when they leave. But the truth is, the real party is underway at home—precisely where they're going. They're not the ones missing the party; those of us left behind are. (Fortunately, if we know Jesus, we'll get there eventually.)

Every person reading this is dying. Perhaps you have reason to believe death will come very soon. You may be troubled, feeling uncertain, or unready to leave. Make sure of your relationship with Jesus Christ. Be certain that you're trusting Him alone to save you—not anyone or anything else, and certainly not any good works you've done. Then allow yourself to get excited about what's on the other side of death's door.

We're going to a beautiful, though temporary, place where we'll await the culmination of history: the return of the risen Jesus who will resurrect us. Then we'll join Him in ruling the New Earth, free of sin and the curse.

INCENTIVES FOR RIGHTEOUS LIVING

The world to come is what we were made for—and it gives shape and meaning to our present lives. If we think regularly of the heavenly and the eternal, we aren't easy prey for Satan's lies and distractions.

Knowing this present world will end and be resurrected into a new heavens and New Earth should profoundly affect our daily behavior.

What did Peter tell us to do in 1 Peter 3:11-14?

_____

_____

If we understand what the phrase "a new heaven and a new earth" means, we will look forward to it. And if we're not looking forward to it, we must not yet understand it. Anticipating our homecoming will motivate us to live spotless lives here and now. Recognizing our future life on a resurrected Earth can help empower us to stick with a difficult marriage, or the hard task of caring for an ailing parent or child, or stay with a demanding job.

Describe a time when you have been faithful to God because you looked forward to His reward.

_____

_____

Knowing where we're going and what rewards we'll receive there directly affects Christ-centered righteous living today. After all, if we really believe we're going to live forever in a realm where Christ, who brings us joy, is the center and that righteous living will mean happiness for all, why wouldn't we choose to get a head start on Heaven through Christ-centered righteous living now?

A LIFE THAT GETS US READY

If my wedding date is on the calendar and I'm thinking of the person I'm going to marry, I shouldn't be an easy target for seduction. Likewise, when I've meditated on Heaven, sin is terribly unappealing. It's when my mind drifts from Heaven that sin seems attractive. Thinking of Heaven leads inevitably to pursuing holiness. Our high tolerance for sin testifies of our failure to prepare for Heaven.

Do you believe that last statement? Why or why not?

_____

_____

Heaven should affect our activities and ambitions, our recreation and friendships, and the way we spend our money and time. If I believe I'll spend eternity in a world of unending beauty and adventure, will I be content to spend all my evenings staring at game shows, sitcoms, and ball games? Even if I keep my eyes off of impurities, how much time will I want to invest in what doesn't matter?

God's Word and people last forever. Spending time in God's Word and investing in people will pay off in eternity and bring me joy and perspective now. Following Christ is not a call to abstain from gratification but to delay gratification. It's finding our joy in Christ rather than seeking joy in the things of this world. Heaven—our assurance of eternal gratification and fulfillment—should be our north star, reminding us where we are and which direction to go.

When we realize the pleasures that await us in God's presence, we can forgo lesser pleasures now. When we realize the possessions that await us in Heaven, we will gladly give away possessions on earth to store up treasures in Heaven. When we realize the power offered to us as rulers in God's kingdom, a power we could not handle now but will handle with benevolence then, we can forgo the pursuit of power here.

To be Heaven oriented is to be goal oriented in the best sense. Paul said, "One thing I do: Forgetting what is behind and straining toward what is ahead, I press on toward the goal to win the prize for which God has called me heavenward in Christ Jesus" (Phil. 3:13-14).

Thinking of Heaven will motivate us to live each day in profound thankfulness to God: "Therefore, since we are receiving a kingdom that cannot be shaken, let us be thankful, and so worship God acceptably with reverence and awe" (Heb. 12:28).

> Heaven should be our north star, reminding us where we are and which direction to go.

ALL THINGS MADE NEW

The most ordinary moment on the New Earth will be greater than the most perfect moments in this life—those experiences you wanted to bottle or hang on to but couldn't. Life on the New Earth will be like sitting in front of the fire with family and friends, basking in the warmth, laughing outrageously, dreaming of the adventures to come—and then going out and living those adventures together with no fear that life will ever end or that tragedy will descend like a dark cloud.

At the climax of the Bible, John recorded: "Now the dwelling of God is with men, and he will live with them. They will be his people, and God himself will be with them and be their God. He will wipe every tear from their eyes. There will be no more death or mourning or crying or pain, for the old order of things has passed away." He who was seated on the throne said, 'I am making everything new!'" (Rev. 21:3-5).

These are the words of King Jesus. Count on them. Take them to the bank. Live every day in light of them. Make every choice in light of Christ's certain promise. We were all made for a person and a place. Jesus is the person. Heaven is the place.

If you know Jesus, I'll be with you in that resurrected world. With the Lord we love and with the friends we cherish, we'll embark together on the ultimate adventure, in a spectacular new universe awaiting our exploration and dominion. Jesus will be the center of all things, and joy will be the air we breathe.

And right when we think it doesn't get any better than this—it will.

1. Wayne Grudem, *Systematic Theology: An Introduction to Biblical Doctrine* (Grand Rapids: Zondervan, 1994), endnote on 1162.
2. Colleen McDannell and Bernhard Lang, *Heaven: A History* (New York: Vintage Books, 1988), 307.
3. James M. Campbell, *Heaven Opened* (New York: Revell, 1924), 123.
4. Martin Luther, "QuoteWorld" [online], [cited 7 August 2006]. Available from the Internet: www.quoteworld.org/quotes/8540.
5. C. S. Lewis, *Letters to Malcolm: Chiefly on Prayer* (New York: Harcourt Brace Jovanovich, 1963), 92-93.

LEADER GUIDE

By Sheila E. Moss

Thank you for leading a study of *Heaven*. This guide will help you set up and lead the study. It includes tips for training facilitators if you have more than one group. Use the suggestions to facilitate the group, start discussions, and keep discussions focused. You will need to review the member material each week. From the study, select the questions that fit your group and lead to productive discussion. Add your own questions as needed. We have provided some extra questions in each day's study. They appear marked with an asterisk.

About the Study

Heaven pulls us from "that's what I've always thought" to confront us with what God has to say about His Heaven. We'll be challenged to examine what we believe and why we believe it. The Scriptures will lead us to think in a way most of us have never considered. Acquiring knowledge about Heaven is not enough, however. We need to make changes in our earthly lives and attitudes.

Plan for one introductory session and six weeks of daily independent study. Each day should take 30-45 minutes to complete. Group participants gather weekly to discuss what they've learned and applied to their lives from their independent study. Arrange for fellowship before or after the discussion.

Beginning a Bible Study Group

Promote the group study of *Heaven* in your church and community using posters, the church's weekly bulletin and newsletter, e-mail announcements, or whatever media to which you have access. Announcements should include meeting time, place, registration opportunities, information about childcare, and at least one contact person and phone number. Using registration responses, plan for small groups of no more than 12 participants. Pre-planning gives a tremendous boost to participation and course effectiveness.

- Pray for God's leading and provision. Ask for His help in all arrangements, including inviting people who have a hunger for His Word and a willingness to study.
- Discuss the course with your pastor and leadership, asking for their help.
- Reserve your meeting place and time. Provide a room with comfortable seating.
- Arrange for childcare if needed.
- Enlist a facilitator for each group.
- Order member books for group members and facilitators.
- Decide whether and when to have refreshments or coffee. Enlist volunteers to organize, prepare, and clean up.

Training Facilitators

Host a training session for your facilitators and give them clear expectations and guidelines. During the training session have each facilitator make name tags for their group members or suggest they provide materials for the members to make their own during the introductory session. Making name tags can provide time for group members to get to know each other and to express their creativity.

Name Tag Tip: Staple ribbons onto index cards, and add pins in the ribbon to make name tags. If participants make their name tags, provide markers or colored pencils for designing the tags along with the cards with attached ribbons and pins. Participants can decorate their own, wear them during the study, and use them as a bookmark throughout the study.

During the training session, acquaint facilitators with "what-to-do-if-situations" and provide general guidelines to address them. Consider what to do if you encounter any of the following:

- a facilitator becomes ill
- prayer time takes up too much time
- group time habitually exceeds the set time
- social time takes away from Bible study
- members habitually come unprepared
- one member dominates group discussion
- one member habitually arrives late to group or leaves early
- members hesitate to share
- members take the discussion far off topic
- member disagrees with content or facilitator

Suggestions for Group Guidelines

Help curtail difficult scenarios within a group by considering the following guidelines in addition to whatever the facilitators determine:

- Respect the responses of all participants but steer a member back on course if the answer goes far from the topic or becomes too lengthy. Try to enlist responses from all participants in the group.
- Decide if, how, and when you will have group prayer time. One option is to have members write out their requests, deposit them into a basket, and ask other members to draw out a request and pray for that specific request during the week.
- If a member tends to dominate the group, ask, "Does anyone else have a comment?" If the member continues to dominate, consider meeting with them after the study. Enlist their aid to draw others into the discussion. Gentleness will often help a dominating member become respectful of others.
- Establish a group schedule and honor it. Begin and end on time, regardless of how many are present. Keeping this schedule encourages members to come on time and respects the efforts of those who are on time.

This course is ideal for a weekday or a weeknight study. It can be used as an outreach Bible study because people have an interest in Heaven. Use it also for the church's discipleship training or other small-group ministry. Adjust the schedule to fit your group.

Responsibilities of Facilitators

Success rests largely with the facilitator. Give attention to the following responsibilities.

PRAY

Pray for your group as a whole; for individual members; for your leading; for participants' attention, study time, and discussion time; and that the results of this study will bring changed lives and attitudes.

BE ON TIME AND PREPARED

Set an example of honoring participants' time by beginning and ending the group on time. Be prepared to facilitate the group—they will know if you are trying to wing it.

ESTABLISH A SAFE GROUP

Establish a safe learning environment. Do not allow one person to intimidate others or dominate the group. You may already have the skills to deal with these challenges, or you may need to work on them.

You are not required to lead perfectly! Follow the Lord's leading and rely on His strength and wisdom. Read the material, prepare your questions, write transitional phrases for moving from one section to another, listen to each response by group members, and respond kindly while maintaining control.

INFORM THE GROUP

Let the group know you will be guiding them through the material they have studied, that you will be calling their attention to some but not all of the questions they have answered.

Make sure they understand that you will not lecture. They need to know you will facilitate. Everyone in the group will learn together—including you.

ANTICIPATE SURPRISES

If participants ask questions you cannot answer, remind them that you are facilitating and learning along with them. Encourage them to study God's Word for answers to their questions and commit to do the same if you can honor that commitment. Point them to the trade book version of *Heaven* for further study. (See p. 160 for more information.)

READ, STUDY, FACILITATE

You will want to read the material, answer the questions in each day's study before meeting with your group. Choose the questions you will ask. In this Leader Guide an asterisk (*) indicates questions that refer to thought questions for which members may not have written answers.

Prepare transitional phrases or statements to move participants from one question or section to the next. Call out the page number for the question you are asking so that members can follow your leading without confusion.

INTRODUCTORY SESSION

GREET & REGISTER PARTICIPANTS

Personally greet all participants. Direct them to a registration table where you have name tags ready. If you prefer, plan for participants to make name tags as they enter and take a seat. This activity can be a way for members to get to know each other. Have registration forms available or have members fill in their names, addresses, phone numbers, and e-mail addresses on a sheet of paper. Make member books available on the table with a basket for collecting the cost of the books. You might want to have them check off their names after they've paid for their books.

Begin promptly at the announced time.

INTRODUCTIONS

Briefly introduce yourself and have participants introduce themselves, giving an adjective that describes their personality.

WELCOMING COMMENTS

Carefully phrase the questions you ask. For example, to begin the Introductory Session, you might

- Thank participants for their attendance, promptness, and sharing their creative personality adjectives
- Welcome members to the course
- Pay particular attention to newcomers from the community or church
- Reiterate the subject of this course, Heaven
- Acquaint group members with the concept of a five-day study format for the purpose of encouraging daily Bible study

GUIDELINES FOR GROUP

In a friendly, gracious voice comment about the procedures (guidelines) for having a smooth comfortable group discussion:

- Instruct the group to respect the responses of all participants.
- Explain that group members commit to working the weekly homework and to sharing from a studied position with the Holy Spirit's leading. They refrain from answering if they have not done their homework.
- Clarify prayer time and when and how it will occur. Stress that prayer requests must be treated with confidentiality.

GROUP SCHEDULE

Tell participants you will honor and protect their time by following the schedule by beginning and ending on time. Explain the group schedule with beginning and ending times.

OVERVIEW OF COURSE

Move the group into further introduction by asking them to open their books to the Table of Contents. To reinforce the vision of the course, point out the weekly titles. Guide them through a quick overview of the study.

The goal of this course is to understand these issues by studying God's Word. Applying the learning to our lives and attitudes can make the difference in whether or not we are looking forward to Heaven. How we live on this earth gets us ready for the New Earth.

FUN PRETEND POP-TEST

Pretend you are a teacher giving a pop-test. Provide participants with paper and pen or pencil if needed. Ask students to number their papers from 1-10. Ask the following questions with exaggeration, urging students to "keep their eyes on their own papers" and please "no talking." Allow time for each response.

1. Define Heaven.
2. Define Paradise.
3. How did you learn what you know about Heaven?
4. Where is Heaven?
5. Is Heaven a real place?
6. Are you looking forward to Heaven?
7. If so, why? If not, why not?
8. How do you know you are going to Heaven?
9. Draw a picture of what you think Heaven looks like.
10. What do you want to get from this study?

This exercise will help participants identify some of what they know about Heaven and how they know it. Hopefully, they will be encouraged to begin the week's study immediately! Tell members you won't take up their papers today, but ask them to keep them to compare with what they learn later.

DISMISSAL

After the quiz, mention that these issues are only some of the points in the course. Thank participants for their interest in Heaven.

Dismiss the group with prayer for diligent reading, studying, and thinking about Heaven.

WEEK 1
Realizing Our Destiny

WELCOME, PRAYER, & TRANSITION

Express your appreciation for the members' accomplishment of having completed a week's study about Heaven. Recognize that they will have many observations to share. Mention that they enrich each week's discussion by their reading and study. Graciously ask group members who have not done the homework to refrain from commenting but to listen to what others contribute to the discussion. One of the main points of group Bible study is to learn from each other from a studied position led by the Holy Spirit.

Reinforce the vision of this week's study as you read each day's title.

Day 1 » *Are You Looking Forward to Heaven?*
Begin today's discussion by asking the following general questions, pausing long enough for members to think about their responses. There are no specific right or wrong answers to this day's questions. Encourage participation in a safe environment. Welcome and value members' comments even though opinions may vary. Watch your time carefully so you can cover the material and still honor your time commitment.

Remember that an asterisk denotes extra questions to which members have not written answers.

• How have you learned what you know about Heaven?*
• What do you think when you read or hear the word *destiny* (p. 7)?*
• How can you determine if you have inaccurate ideas about Heaven? How can you correct inaccurate ideas (p. 10)?*
• If you were truly to long for Heaven, how might your life change (p. 11)?

Day 2 » *Is Heaven Beyond Our Imagination?*

- Why does our culture fear and deny death (p. 12)?
- Have you ever done an extensive study of Heaven? Could there be Scriptures about Heaven you've never read or paid particular attention to?*
- How should you approach any teaching of God's Word? (Read Acts 17:11; 1 Thess. 5:21; and 1 John 4:1-3.)*
- How would you answer the person who insists it's wrong to imagine Heaven as a physical place (p. 13)?

Day 3 » *Is It OK to Imagine Heaven as a Literal Place?*

- How do we know it's OK to study and talk about Heaven (p. 17)?
- Do you know when someone is misquoting Scripture? Do you know if or when you misquote Scripture (p. 17)?
- Why do you think God orders us to think deeply about Heaven (p. 18)?

Day 4 » *Is Heaven Our Default Destination?*

- What is your response to the statement, "We should be shocked not that some people could go to hell but that any would be permitted into Heaven" (p. 21)?*
- What did Jesus say about hell (p. 22)?*
  Matthew 10:28
  Matthew 13:40-42
  Mark 9:43-44
- Why do we not tell unsaved people about the cancer of sin and evil? Why do we not tell them about the inevitable penalty of eternal destruction and that eternal destruction can be avoided by Jesus Christ's atoning sacrifice (pp. 23-24)?
- What does the statement "Earth is an in-between world" mean (p. 24)?*

Day 5 » *Can You Know You're Going to Heaven?*

- When did you RSVP to Jesus' invitation to Heaven?*
- If you haven't responded to His RSVP, why are you ignoring it? Do you know how to respond to His invitation (pp. 28-30)?

Special Significance

What other Scriptures, statements, questions, or comments in this week's study are of special significance to you?

Dismiss the group with prayer, asking God for discerning hearts open to learning what He wants us to know this week.

WEEK 2
Understanding the Present Heaven

WELCOME, PRAYER, & TRANSITION

Give a one-sentence summary or mention the topics of each day's study. Have participants look at headings of week 2 to set the scene, to focus the group, and to help participants recall what they studied about understanding the present Heaven.

Day 1 » *What Is the Present Heaven?*

- What excites, interests, or confuses you about the teaching of the present Heaven (p. 32)?
- Read Hebrews 13:8. Why might some people use this verse to argue against the idea of present Heaven (p. 34)?
- Explain the different states of Heaven as presented by Randy Alcorn (p. 35).

Day 2 » *What Is the Significance of the Future Heaven?*

- What is the significance of the future Heaven (p. 36)?*
- What is the significance of the New Jerusalem (p. 37)?*
- What is the River of Life (p. 38)?*
- What is the Tree of Life (p. 39)?*
- If given a choice, would you choose to have no needs or to have all your needs met and why (p. 39)?

Day 3 » *Is the Present Heaven a Physical Place?*

- Why do you think the present Heaven is or is not a physical place (p. 40)? *
- What do you think "Heaven as substance, Earth as shadow" means (p. 42)? *
- What do you think about the concept that "the present Heaven is paradise" (p. 43)? *
- What occupations would you like to try if you weren't prevented by lack of time or opportunity (p. 44)?

Day 4 » *Do People Have Bodies in the Present Heaven?*

- Why do you think people will or will not have bodies in the present Heaven (p. 45)?*
- What did you learn about the rich man and Lazarus (pp. 46-47)?*

Day 5 » *What Is Life Like in the Present Heaven?*

- Which of these listed observations about life in the present Heaven encourage you? Which seem the most difficult to believe (pp. 49-50)?
- What would you say to convince a friend that occupants of Heaven are aware of events on earth (p. 52)?
- How would you explain the statement that "happiness in Heaven is based not on ignorance but on perspective" (p. 52)?

Special Significance

- What other Scriptures, statements, questions, or comments in this week's study are of special significance to you?

Dismiss the group with prayer thanking God for enlightenment and insights about Heaven from His Word. Ask Him for continued persistence in reading, studying, learning, and applying His truth.

WEEK 3
Grasping Redemption's Far Reach

WELCOME, PRAYER, & TRANSITION

Have participants look at headings of week 3 to set the scene and focus the group and to help them recall what they studied about grasping redemption's far reach.

Day 1 » *Why Is Earth's Redemption Essential to God's Plan?*

- When did God instate His earthly renewal plan (p. 54)? *
- What do the words *reconcile, redeem, restore, recover, return, renew, regenerate, resurrect,* and *reclaim* suggest about God (p. 55)? *
- Using Matthew 19:28 and Revelation 21:1, discuss why God's glory demands that He succeed in renewing the earth (pp. 56-57).
- What tangibles did Jesus include in "the renewal of all things" (p. 57)?*
- Why is earth's redemption essential to God's plan (pp. 53-57)?

Day 2 » *Why Is the Resurrection So Important?*

- What excites you most about being restored to God's original design (p. 60)?
- What is crucial about the principle of "continuity of redemption" (pp. 60-61)?
- Why is the resurrection so important (pp. 58-61)?

Day 3 » *What Will It Mean for the Curse to be Lifted?*

- How do you see the removal of the curse changing your life (p. 64)?
- In what ways does Christ reverse the damage done by the first Adam (p. 65)?*
- What do you think about the uniting of Heaven and earth (p. 66)?*
- What will it mean for the curse to be lifted (pp. 63-67)?

Day 4 » *What Does the Restored Earth Mean?*

- How can some Scripture seem to suggest the present earth and universe will be destroyed while others speak of the earth's remaining forever (p. 67)? (See Ps. 78:69; 102:25-26; Eccl. 1:4; 2 Pet. 3:10; Rev. 21:1.)*
- In what way does this review of Scripture cause you to think differently about Heaven (pp. 68-70)?
- How does the "destruction of the earth by flood" in Noah's day help you understand the future "destruction of the earth by fire" (p. 71)? *
- How would you respond to the person who dismisses a future on the New Earth with the claim that the earth will be destroyed (p. 71)?
- What does *the restored earth* mean (pp. 67-71)?

Day 5 » *Will the New Earth Feel Like Home?*

- What do you look forward to doing on the New Earth that you've never gotten to do here (p. 72)?
- What would you respond to a friend who said, "This world is not our home" (p. 74)? *

- What do you love about this present earth (p. 74)? *
- Why will the New Earth feel like home (pp. 72-74)? *

Special Significance

- What other Scriptures, statements, questions, or comments in this week's study are of special significance to you?

Dismiss the group with prayer for diligent study, for participation, and for taking action on what we learn. Ask for relief from confusion for whatever is unclear.

WEEK 4
Celebrating the Joy And Industry of the New Earth

WELCOME, PRAYER, & TRANSITION

Have participants look at headings of week 4 to set the scene and focus the group and to help them recall what they studied about celebrating the joy and industry of the New Earth.

Day 1 » *What Will It Mean to See God?*
- What is God's greatest gift to us (p. 75)? *
- Will we see the faces of both the Father and the Son (p. 76)?
- For those of us who struggle under a persistent cloud of guilt, how might understanding God's joyful nature help us love Him and enjoy His gracious gifts (p. 78)?
- Mention some daily details that bring you joy and a desire to praise God (p. 79).

- What do you think it will mean to see God (pp. 75-79)?

Day 2 » *What Will It Mean for God to Dwell Among Us?*
- What does "the joy of a God-centered Heaven" mean to you? (p. 80). *
- How does wanting to share an accomplishment with someone you love relate to Jesus' words in John 17:24 (p. 81)?*
- Tell about a time when you realized you brought someone else joy (p. 82).
- How do you feel knowing God will serve you (p. 82)? (See Luke 12:37.) *
- In what ways is Jesus already fulfilling this promise to serve you every day (p. 83)?
- What do you imagine when you think of being with God (pp. 83-84)?*

Day 3 » *How Will We Worship God?*
- How do you relate to the statement, "If you've ever had a taste of true worship, you crave more of it, never less" (p. 86)? *
- Revelation 19:8 says, "Fine linen represents the righteous acts of the saints." Why do you suppose the fine linen is comprised of your acts (p. 87)?
- In what ways are you sewing your wedding garment (p. 88)?
- Based on your readings, what is your understanding of how you will worship God in Heaven (pp. 84-88)?*

Day 4 » *Will We Actually Rule with Christ?*

- What experience have you had lately that Christ either has used or could use to prepare you to rule with Him (p. 90)?
- Are you surprised that you'll rule the earth (pp. 90-91)? Why? *
- How do you respond to "owning and ruling the land" (p. 91)? *
- What does Luke 14:11 tell you about leadership positions on the New Earth (p. 92)?
- What dreams might God be preparing you to live out on the New Earth (p. 93)?
- Will you actually rule with Christ (pp. 89-93)?*

Day 5 » *How Will We Rule God's Kingdom?*

- Ask someone to read aloud Romans 12:2, adding the phrase "as it is now, under the curse" (p. 94).
- Describe a time when someone "made the invisible God visible" for you (p. 96).
- How do you feel about "service as a reward" (p. 97)? *
- Who will inherit or possess the kingdom according to the following Scriptures: Matthew 5:3,5,10; 1 Peter 5:5-6 (p. 98).

Special Significance

- What other Scriptures, statements, questions, or comments in this week's study are of special significance to you?

Dismiss the group, praying words of encouragement for faithfulness in attendance, for lesson preparation, and for sharing what God has taught us. Pray for endurance to complete the course.

WEEK FIVE
What Will Our Lives Be Like in Heaven?

WELCOME, PRAYER, & TRANSITION

To transition from week 4, have participants look at headings of week 5 to set the scene and focus the group and to help them recall what they studied about what our lives will be Like in heaven.

Day 1: Should *We Expect to Maintain Our Own Identities?*

- Do you expect to retain your individuality in Heaven (p. 99)? Why or why not?*
- What do you think is the strongest reason to believe you will retain your individuality in Heaven (p. 100)?
- Describe a time you really felt good about yourself, not in pride or arrogance, but when you sensed you honored God, helped the needy, were faithful, humble, and servant-hearted, like Jesus (p. 101).
- In Heaven will you be called by your present name (pp. 102-103)?*
- What does "be perfect" mean (pp. 103-104)?*

Day 2 » *What Will Our Bodies Be Like?*

- What do you think about experiencing hunger in Heaven (p. 106)?*
- What does Revelation 7:16 suggest about thirst on the New Earth (p. 106)?
- What does Galatians 3:25-29 teach about gender in Heaven (pp. 107-108)?

• Will you wear clothes in the present and future Heaven (p. 108)? *

Day 3 » *What Will a Typical Day Be Like?*

• What do you love to do under the category of active rest (p. 109)?

• Do you think you will sleep on the New Earth (p. 110)? *

• Will you work in Heaven (pp. 110-111)? *

• What do John 4:34 and 5:17 suggest about being like the Father and Jesus (p. 110)?

• What will you do for eternity to glorify God (p. 111)? *

• What will a typical day be like on the New Earth (pp. 109-111)?*

Day 4 » *What Will Our Relationships Be Like?*

• Read 1 Thessalonians 4:14,17. What did Paul say about reunion in Heaven (p. 113)?*

• Will we recognize each other (pp. 113-114)?* (Consider John 20:15-16 and Luke 24:15-16.)

• Do you think there will be marriage, families, and friendships in Heaven (pp. 114-116)? *

Day 5 » *What Will We Experience Together?*

• What is the significance of the way people in Heaven respond to God's judgments (see Rev. 18:20; p. 118)?

• What will it mean to share discoveries together in Heaven (pp. 119-120)? *

• Describe a time when you uniquely bonded with a group because of an experience you shared (p. 119).

• Read aloud Luke 6:21-23. How could Jesus' words confirm Randy's statements on pages 121-122?

Special Significance

• What other Scriptures, statements, questions, or comments in this week's study are of special significance to you?

Dismiss the group with prayer asking for perseverance and inquisitive minds to search God's truths about His Heaven and to apply them to our lives.

WEEK 6
What Will We Do in Heaven?

WELCOME, PRAYER,
& TRANSITION

To transition from the previous lesson, give a one-sentence summary or mention the topics of each day's study.

Day 1 » *What Will We Know and Learn?*

• Read Ephesians 2:6-7. How do you know you will continue to learn in Heaven (p. 124)?*

• What genuine obstacles now prevent you from actively seeking all the new knowledge and better understanding you'd like (p. 125)?

• About what events do you particularly long to hear "the rest of the story" (p. 125)?

• Describe a time you felt particular satisfaction because you learned something (p. 127).

Day 2 » *Will Work Be Engaging? Will We Express Creativity?*

• What type of work do you find most satisfying, and how might it be enhanced on the New Earth (pp. 128-129)?

• What does Isaiah 65:21 specifically tell us we'll do in the New Earth (p. 130)?

- Scan Exodus 25–40 (specifically 31–36). How do you know God values craftsmanship (pp. 130-131)? *
- What does Romans 11:29 tell you about God's gifts and calling and what does that have to do with technology and machinery in Heaven (p. 131)?

Day 3 » *Will There Be Arts, Entertainment, and Sports?*

- What role will music play in Heaven (see Rev. 14:2-3 and John 8:7-13 and 15:2, p. 133)? *
- What does Revelation 21:1-4 suggest about stories in Heaven (p. 134)? *
- Pretend you are on a debate team. How would you argue the case that there will be laughter in Heaven? (Luke 6:21,23, pp. 134-135)? *
- If you really reflected on the great joy of your Lord (Neh. 8:10; Luke 6:21), how would your attitude change (p. 135)?
- How do you react to the idea of sports in Heaven (pp. 135-136)?
- What concepts about Heaven have you rethought this week and what difference does it make (p. 138)?

Day 4 » *Will Our Dreams Be Fulfilled and Missed Opportunities Regained?*

- Name three dreams you look forward to fulfilling in Heaven, and tell why one of them is most important to you (p. 139).
- What difference does all this reading and study and information about Heaven make to you (p. 142)?*

Day 5 » *Are You Living in Light of Heaven?*

- If Alcorn's party illustration were a parable, how would you explain it (pp. 142-143)?
- How can an enthusiastic anticipation of Heaven help us to do what 1 Peter 3:11-14 tells us to do (p. 144)?
- Describe a time when you have been faithful to God because you looked forward to His reward (p. 144).
- What about your life here on earth is getting you ready for Heaven (pp. 144-145)? *
- According to Revelation 21:3-5, what does God do with all things (p. 146)? *

Special Significance

- What other Scriptures, statements, questions, or comments in this week's study are of special significance to you?

Dismiss the group with a prayer of gratitude for God's revelation of His Heaven, the gift of Himself, and for believers who look forward to Heaven.

Consider a celebration to conclude your time together as a group. You might all have a meal together or a dessert fellowship. Allow time for each person to share what the group meant to him or her. Invite each member to add to a list of persons to enlist for another study. Consider together what your group can do next better to be better prepared for ministry in the light of our future in Heaven.

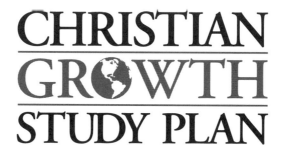

CHRISTIAN GROWTH STUDY PLAN

In the Christian Growth Study Plan *Heaven* is a resource for course credit in the subject area Bible Studies in the Christian Growth category of diploma plans. To receive credit, read the book; complete the learning activities; attend group sessions; show your work to your pastor, a staff member, or a church leader; then complete the form. This page may be duplicated. Send the completed form to:

Christian Growth Study Plan, One LifeWay Plaza, Nashville, TN 37234-0117; Fax (615) 251-5067; e-mail *cgspnet@lifeway.com*. For information about the Christian Growth Study Plan, refer to the current *Christian Growth Study Plan Catalog*, located online at *www.lifeway.com/cgsp*. If you do not have access to the Internet, contact the Christian Growth Study Plan office, (800) 968-5519, for the specific plan needed for your ministry.

HEAVEN
Course Number: CG-1229

PARTICIPANT INFORMATION

Social Security Number (USA ONLY-optional) | Personal CGSP Number* | Date of Birth (MONTH, DAY, YEAR)

Name (First, Middle, Last) | Home Phone

Address (Street, Route, or P.O. Box) | City, State, or Province | Zip/Postal Code

Email Address for CGSP use

Please check appropriate box: ❑ Resource purchased by church ❑ Resource purchased by self ❑ Other

CHURCH INFORMATION

Church Name

Address (Street, Route, or P.O. Box) | City, State, or Province | Zip/Postal Code

CHANGE REQUEST ONLY

☐ Former Name

☐ Former Address | City, State, or Province | Zip/Postal Code

☐ Former Church | City, State, or Province | Zip/Postal Code

Signature of Pastor, Conference Leader, or Other Church Leader | Date

*New participants are requested but not required to give SS# and date of birth. Existing participants, please give CGSP# when using SS# for the first time. Thereafter, only one ID# is required. **Mail to:** Christian Growth Study Plan, One LifeWay Plaza, Nashville, TN 37234-0117. Fax: (615)251-5067.

Revised 4-05